Vivienne –

With all Love and

Gratitude –

March '89

· THE WEB ·

BOOKS BY ANDREW HARVEY

◆

POETRY

Winter Scarecrow
Masks and Faces
Evidence
Homage to Toukaram
The Fabius Poems
A Full Circle
No Diamonds, No Hat, No Honey

TRANSLATIONS
(with Anne Pennington)

Macedonian Songs
Blazhe Konesky (*Selected Poems*)
The Golden Apple

FICTION

One Last Mirror
Burning Houses
The Web

NONFICTION
A Journey in Ladakh

THE WEB

❖

ANDREW HARVEY

❖

HOUGHTON MIFFLIN COMPANY

BOSTON · 1987

LIBRARY OF CONGRESS CATALOGING-IN-PUBLICATION DATA

Harvey, Andrew, date.
The web.
I. Title.
PR6058.A6986W4   1987   823'.914   86-27408
ISBN 0-395-42921-8

PRINTED IN THE UNITED STATES OF AMERICA

S 10 9 8 7 6 5 4 3 2 1

The author is grateful for permission to quote lines from *The Conference of the Birds* by Farid ud-Din Attar, translated by C. S. Nott. Copyright © 1954 by C. S. Nott. Reprinted by arrangement with Shambhala Publications, Inc., 314 Dartmouth Street, Boston, Massachusetts 02116.

Nikandra's

"Near the day of purification
there will be cobwebs
spun back and forth in the sky"

·ONE·

The letter arrived in early October on a Paris morning so full and clear I had no desire to open it but let it lie on my desk until lunchtime soaking up the autumn sun. I can see it now—with its willful but straggly handwriting, its brown, still slightly scented envelope, its lines of canceled addresses and overlaid postmarks. It had followed me to several places, and finally tracked me down. How dare it find me, I remember thinking, *here* of all places when I feel finally out of the wind? "Out of the wind?" I can hear Adolphe laughing. "The desire to be out of the wind is even more dangerous than the wind itself. Makes one dull, makes one dumb . . ."

I had moved out of Anna's Venetian jewelbox of a flat in the rue Jacob, into a smaller apartment she had found me in the rue de l'Université. Anna called it my zenling, mockingly, because it was white and empty and looked out across a cobblestone courtyard onto a large rough high stone wall, and because I had refused to put any furniture in it besides two black chairs, a big black bed with a black bedspread, and a white desk with nothing on it but a vase and a typewriter. Adolphe visited it only once ("I have an instinct, pondsnipe, that it will be far too small for me"), but in high Adolphine style. Wearing pink plastic slippers, a black velvet dress, décolleté, with

3

a long black satin train spangled with stars, he cast one glance round the room, shrieked "It's a coffin, darling, a *coffin*," and ran back down the stairs, startling the concierge's fat and noisy black poodle, who had never seen anything quite like him and began to bark hysterically. Whatever Adolphe might think of my room, it suited me. It was calm and I was beginning to write again after a silence.

Not that I had much time for writing in those days. Most of my hours were spent with Adolphe, who was dying in his flat in Saint Sulpice. "How are you today?" I would say, coming through his white doors in the morning. "Dying beautifully," he would reply. "Dying *exemplarily*. How my dear departed dreadful mother would have loved it could she have lived to see it—she who lived in terror that I would be knifed by a matelot and dumped in the Seine and she would have to go and identify me. What *would* she wear for the morgue? Diamonds too showy, pearls a little unfeeling?"

It was difficult often to believe Adolphe was dying at all. He talked, laughed, cooked, dressed up, drove around, laughed, telephoned, so much (and so exhaustingly) it was tempting sometimes to think that the hollows that were deepening in his cheeks, the sudden glaring thinness of his wrists, his fits of coughing and prostration, were all parts of a new role, hooks, sequins and buttons and velvet patches for a stunning new costume. Adolphe was setting about dying, as he said himself often, "like a sort of transvestite Lady Hester Stanhope going on a trek," making lists of the ten favorite foods and books he would take with him (how they altered! Only mangoes, Firbank, and the Diamond Sutra were constants). He spent his time writing, for the first time in his life, long letters to friends, full of pleas to admit that Orson Welles was no good, to promise him that when he did, if he did, finally "pop it," they would never wear Opium or eat things fried too long or settle in Australia. He was never more thrilling than in those days, or more sententious, or more annoying. Whether he knew it or not, he demanded all my time, and I was happy to give it. Adolphe made his dying the longest party of his life.

For Anna that early autumn was a time of appraisal, nervousness, and farewell. She was preparing to go to India for the winter. She was packing up her flat. She had been to India at the end of the sixties with her then husband. Now she felt driven to go again, to take stock of everything, "to break with the old Anna who is boring me to death. I'm going to leave her, you'll see, in a battered trunk at Delhi airport with no identifying papers." She packed up her flat with a ghoulish joy at burying the past. "That's the sixties over," she would shout, stamping—before I could stop her—on two pink Kashmir boxes. "That's the end of *him*," she would laugh, throwing a copy of *Joseph and His Brothers* that Hans, her "last," had given her, out of the window. "He wasn't even bright enough to know I can't *stand* biblical themes." She had bravely decided to give up writing "trashy songs" for a living and survive in India on her last remaining capital. She was nervous about what the future might bring: "I'm thirty-nine and the sun wrinkles . . ."

Adolphe's dying and Anna's departure: both absorbed and disturbed me. I wanted to stay in Paris to be with my friends, to give what help I could. I wanted to stay in my room, small and odd though it was. The letter,

5

from a part of my past I had thought closed for several years, was the last thing I wanted.

Anna, over the phone: "Read Richard's mother's letter to me."

"I can't do her voice. I never met her. I heard about her, of course. Her Chinese laundryman lovers, her affair with the Great Poet who called her Chloe— Chloe, for god's sake—in his long rambling adulterous poems . . ."

"You know the upper-class Boston voice by now, surely, the speaking as if through freshly scrubbed teeth. Read it. I've just thrown away all the Hermann Hesses that Hans gave me and feel ready for anything."

"'Charles,'" I began in a high would-be Boston drawl. "God, these American aristos are direct. Not even a 'dear Charles,' or a fake 'dearest.' When they want something, they say so.

"'Charles, I think you can imagine how little I like writing to you and asking for your help. We never met but what I knew of you I was suspicious of and did not like. And nothing I have read of yours has changed my mind. I prefer more reticent writing, more Mozartian.'"

"Good god."

"'But now I need your help. I need it badly. In fact I believe only you can help . . .'"

"Oh god," said Anna, "how I hate people that say 'Only you can help.' I always feel like saying, 'Look, I can hardly cross a road without nearly being run over.'"

"'No, I am *certain* only you can help.'"

"Doesn't sound Mozartian to me."

"'My son has disappeared. He went into Mount Vernon asylum just outside Boston, as you know, and spent

6

a year there. I do not know whether he was in contact with you, but all his doctors said he was cured. He came back two months ago to live with me.'"

"Back to Jocasta," Anna said. "The idiot."

"'He came back two months ago to live with me—'" I repeated.

"Don't go on," said Anna. "Let me guess. Richard told her the Awful Truth at last, that he was in love with you and that she and the rest of the family could go fuck itself. He tried to kill her under the family portrait of Granny. He burnt the house down, hoping she was in it, but actually at the time she was in Maine in the arms of the Great Poet who was beating out hexameters on her back."

"'—and now has disappeared, and I am afraid for his life.'"

Anna whistled. "*Now* she is afraid?"

"'I am afraid for his life and I think only you can find him and speak to him. He spoke to me so much of you in these last months. You and I must talk now. I am going to ask of you a great, a vast favor. I am going to ask you to come to America and find Richard. I have enclosed a check which should more than cover expenses.'"

"How much?" Anna asked.

"Anna, really . . . how *vulgar*."

"Better vulgar than crazy. Charles, promise me you are not going. Swear that you will not go back into all that. You did what you could for Richard. He nearly did you in. You're over him. Write Jocasta she can go and hire another private detective. Adolphe needs you here in Paris. I need you. Who else is going to help me carry my suitcases to the airport? Who else am I going to cling to like Lillian Gish when the time comes to go up those steps and away into the new life? You can't go."

7

"I haven't made up my mind."

"I know that voice . . . What do you think you can *do*? Wander around America on Greyhound buses looking for a James Dean look-alike who might be anywhere between Dallas and Syracuse? Charles, you have a room in Paris. A white bare room. Stay in it. Fester sweetly. Watch the birds come and go on that stone wall of yours. Take up yoga in the afternoons. I know a swami with the most delicious eyebrows . . ."

I started laughing. "Would you take your own advice? I loved Richard."

"I loved Hans. I loved a gardener with one eye once. I loved several megalomaniacs in succession, as you well know. Love is no bloody excuse for putting your peace of mind and heart in peril. You are *not* responsible for Richard's going mad. You might like to think you are. It might give you a *frisson* of devilishness . . . but that boy was a vase cracked from the beginning. And cracked by guess who. You have paid your dues to Love. I remember you during that long awful summer when he went mad. I had to put up with you and see you ate and didn't hit people at parties. Remember?"

"I'm not likely to forget."

"Promise me one thing," Anna said wearily. "You won't reply until you've had a long talk with Adolphe."

"You're hoping he'll do one of his marvelous death scenes and move me into staying and posting all those crazy long letters of his."

"That's exactly what I'm hoping. Redeeming the American boy is a fantasy. You cannot redeem him or yourself or it. It's a sort of vulgar nineteen fifties nonsense to think you can."

"Why are you going back to India, then?"

8

"I'm not going to India to redeem anything. I'm going to India to make friends with my own spirit. I hate the word *redeem* anyway. My mother used to use it a lot just after she'd had one of her fits and tried to strangle me in my sleep. I'm going to India to buy a lot of blue silk saris and sit by the sea."

"Liar."

"Don't let that woman flatter you into surrendering your peace."

"*What* peace?"

Anna laughed. "What peace, indeed?" Then she said, "I'm not going to India to find peace. I don't give a fig for peace, actually. I want to *dance,* for a change. My god, I *am* sounding banal. I'll ring off before I start singing Krishna songs and staring off into space. Ring me when you've seen Adolphe and come to your senses."

"Come to your senses . . ." I was determined to stay in my senses, determined not to let the letter shake me.

And then, involuntarily, I remembered with complete clarity Richard's and my first meeting.

"Well, this is a surprise."

Adolphe was sitting with his feet tucked up under him on his Louis Quinze sofa. The small, grinning sphinxes stuck along it seemed particularly amused this evening. The sofa was surrounded by small butter-lamps which made Adolphe seem almost unreal, his face with its dark rings under the eyes swimming in and out of the light.

There was nothing unreal about his laugh.

"Oh, Charlie, I love it. You always dreaming of the Quiet Life and life always taking away any scrap of quiet you might have won. Aren't you being told something? You haven't said anything about my costume."

Adolphe was dressed in a vast black kimono painted with phosphorescent skulls. From each of the skulls dangled a flower.

"It's certainly startling."

"Can't you do any better than that? *Startling*? You sound like one of those women at an English tea party. The news from Lebanon is very *startling*, isn't it? All these reports of necrophilia on the Underground are very *startling*, aren't they? *Startling* is not a word one uses in *this* room."

Adolphe waved imperiously in the air—a wave that took in the four large Buddhas in the corners, the chandelier above us with its strips of saffron, the great black marble tear still glistening from its libation of Ganges water.

Then he coughed raucously. "You'd think I was acting, wouldn't you? Clutching my throat and spitting. It's only the real bits in my films that anyone ever found melodramatic. I wouldn't mind dying so much if I didn't have to cough. It ruins my vocal cords and I can no longer sing along with Maria. Do you know what I'm reading now?"

Adolphe had recently discovered reading, as well as writing long wild letters. He had begun to ring all his friends up and say things like "Really Conrad isn't at all bad" or "Proust understands something" and then go into cackles at himself "being serious at last."

"I'm reading about dolphins."

"Dolphins?"

"Don't sound so surprised. I've always had a passion for dolphins."

"First time I've heard of it."

"Well, darling, I can't tell you everything. There are at least sixty years of my life I've told you very little about. Mostly of course because I can't remember them. That's the reward for being so spontaneous. Living in a state of exuberant amnesia. Dolphins are *it*. I've been trying to teach Marlene about dolphins, but she says she's bored with the sea. Bored with the sea! Isn't that marvelous? Perhaps she's eliminating the elements one by one to end in a sort of rapturous stunned nothingness. Do you want to hear my dolphin improvisation?"

"No."

"Don't you even want to hear my imitation of a dolphin coming up for air?"

Before I could stop him Adolphe had leapt up, thrust his head into the air, and started to make very convincing spouting sounds.

He flopped back onto the sofa.

"Of course I'm a dolphin, pondsnipe, and soon" (his voice crackled) "I too will be coming up for air." He smiled at my consternation. "You don't really like it when I refer to the Great Event, do you? It's your English training. Why shouldn't I go on about it? It's fascinating, and it's going to happen, and I'm very much looking forward to what comes after."

Then he said, putting his head on one side, "You're going, of course."

"Going where?"

"Going *where*? You are too much. When the angel of death arrives, you will ask him what the scythe in his hand is for."

"You mean you think I should go to America?"

"*Think*? I'm long past thinking. I *know*. You *must* go. It is necessary. For you, for whatever-his-name-is."

"Richard."

"For Richard. A dull name, but what can one do about that? Not as bad as Kevin, for example, or Chuck. I don't think I would allow you to go for someone called Chuck."

"But Adolphe—"

"I know what you are going to say. That I need you here; that I am popping it—*lovely* expression, sounds like a bottle of champagne!—and I need a witness, a nurse. Darling, with all due respect, that is *rot*. I do not need you here. I love your visits. You don't need me to say that. But I really can manage on my own, and if I get to the state where I'm falling down and ringing up people I don't know, I shall get in a nice Japanese nurse with muscles. The last thing I want to do is to constrain the lives of those I love."

Adolphe's eyes were big with amusement.

"I have a very selfish purpose in asking you to go to America. I've never believed in any of my friends doing anything I don't benefit from. I want you to go so we can have a correspondence."

"What?"

"A correspondence. Letters. Does that turn you on?"

"This new phase of yours is very alarming. I don't think I want any of your letters filled with character analyses and denunciations."

"Those are just for the ordinary friends. We will have something much madder. There is a lot I must tell you and I can only concentrate when I write. How funny to find that I *can* write. For years I've done nothing but talk. Now I want to write. It's such fun typing."

"Especially the way you do it. With no punctuation and no spaces between the words."

"For you I will master punctuation. For you I will put

white spaces between the words. Go to America; write and tell me everything and I'll write and tell you everything. We'll give whatever is happening to each other. There are important things I must tell you that I can't *tell* you—I will have to concentrate and write them down."

"Concentrate, Adolphe? You have the concentration span of a mosquito."

"That's what you think."

"You could write them to me if I stayed here . . ."

"You are not going to stay here. You have to go."

"Oh, for god's sake . . ."

Adolphe stood up, suddenly calm and serious. "Charles, you are frightened. You loved him. Somewhere you still love him. The bleak look in your eyes just now when you told me about the letter told me all I need to know. But remember the letter is only a device, one of life's invitations to the dance."

"What *are* you trying to say?"

"What I see these days I see musically in clusters . . . I can't explain it easily." He began to stroke my neck. "Being very sick," he began, "can be a sort of blessing. I'm not being pious. I'm telling you what I find. Suddenly the walls between things fall down or become transparent. Don't look so baffled. It makes your ears stick out." Adolphe put his head on one side as if listening to something. "Anna is going to India. I am going to god-knows-where. You are now going to America. We are spreading over the earth. The Unholy Trinity is spreading over the earth." He paused, "What a trinity we are! God the Father, an aging transvestite; God the Son, a Garbo-eyed Possessed One with a penchant for ephebes; God the Holy Ghost, a gauloise-voiced demimondaine. Thank god the spirit isn't choosy, and has a sense of humor!"

"I haven't the slightest idea of what you are talking about."

"You will. Before you go—and I suggest you go next week at the same time as Anna—we will have a party. Just the three of us. Not here, though."

"Where?"

"You'll see."

Adolphe started singing "Quando rapita in estasi" from *Lucia*.

"Adolphe, what are you sending me to?"

"I'm not sending you. You are sending yourself. You knew the moment you read the letter that you would have to go." Adolphe paused, and said slowly, "It was when you remembered the first meeting with Richard that you decided."

I stared at him in amazement.

"Don't worry, banana. I don't live in a state of *perpetual* omniscience. Just intermittent. You are going, dear Charles, into the darkness of the past. Keep your sense of humor. Be aware of your splendor. Give Richard this."

"How do you know I'll find him?"

Adolphe laughed and said nothing.

Then he reached into the pocket of his kimono and drew out a ring. It was three rings joined into one, in three types of gold: white, reddish, and yellow.

"Give him this from me . . . from us."

"Cartier. Nineteen fifty-five."

"Fifty-seven. But close. And quite irrelevant."

Anna and I had arranged to meet after my dinner with Adolphe. She was waiting downstairs in the Café La

Mairie, dressed in a simple black skirt with a bright red cashmere sweater, her hair drawn back. It was a sharp starry November evening.

"You're admiring me." She smiled. "Good."

"You look ten years younger since the Hans *débâcle*."

"Death rejuvenates. Just as well. We seem to go through it often enough. So what did the Great White Guava deliver herself of?"

I reconstructed Adolphe's and my conversation.

"He really said that stuff about the Trinity?"

"Yes."

"Perhaps he's losing it."

"I don't think so. He's thin but he looks wonderful."

"And he really did say that about you and your first meeting with Richard?"

"Why should I invent anything?"

"I'm not accusing you. That's too improbable to invent anyway. Or perhaps not. Adolphe's always had that odd gift for reading one's mind. He did once with Hans, you know."

"You never told me."

"It was just before I went to Venice that last time. I visited Adolphe to say goodbye. He looked at me and said, 'Well, darling, read his diary. You'll get his full banality then.' How did he know Hans kept a diary? I didn't until I found it on our bedside table in Venice."

She studied her hands in front of her.

"You've put your wedding ring on again, I see."

"Yes." She looked up. "I decided the other day it was ridiculous not to wear it, even though Peter and I are divorced. For years I couldn't wear it because it reminded me of Peter and of all *that*. Going back to India, to where we were . . ."

"You're going back to the ashram?"

"Oh, not for good. Only for a visit."

"You felt it would be somehow cowardly to go back without your ring."

"I don't know what I felt. I'm wearing it anyhow. Let's change the subject."

She smiled.

"You're being mysterious."

"No, I'm not. I just don't want to talk about India, or Peter, or the ashram, or anything. I want to go and *live* it. I don't want to talk it all away beforehand. Enough of this. Let's have a large stiff wild drink with a little bit of everything in it."

One of Anna's greatest gifts is her command over waiters. She has to raise one finger, like Mrs. Robinson in *The Graduate,* and they come running from unsuspected directions. Tonight's catch was a ruffled gray-haired man in trousers too big for him. He had been drinking; he swayed slightly.

We ordered gondole with tequila, vodka, and gin. The drinks went quickly to our heads.

"You admire my tact, of course," said Anna.

"Your tact?"

"In not talking about Richard. Are all my virtues always to remain hidden?"

"You said quite enough on the phone for me to know exactly what you think."

"But that was yesterday."

"But that was yesterday" is one of Anna's favorite phrases. It sums up for her her right to reinvent herself constantly.

"So what now?"

"Adolphe isn't the only one with premonitions," she said. "I dreamt of you and Richard last night."

"I don't believe you."

"Yes I did. And at length."

I got up. "I don't want to know."

"You really are on the buzz. This business is really getting to you."

"Yes, it is."

"Then sit down and stop being stupid."

The firm voice. I sat down.

"You are not talking about him at all," Anna said. "Why?"

"I'm not sure."

"I think if the letter comes now, then it is for a purpose. You are being led to something."

I groaned.

"Of course you want your room," she went on, "and the rough stone wall and the concierge with the gap teeth and the poodle who plays with decapitated plastic dolls. You *think* you want them, at any rate. You can't have them."

"Why the hell not?"

"Because you are not seventy and you can't play at being seventy. It's all in my dream."

She looked at me quietly to see if I wanted her to go on. "It's not the right time to tell you."

I looked away.

"Did Adolphe tell you about the party?"

"What party?" For the moment I had forgotten.

"The party he's going to give for the two of us before we leave."

"You mean he's told you about the party already?"

Anna smiled.

"So he knew I would go to America?"

Anna shrugged her shoulders and looked at the ceiling.

"Adolphe didn't *write* this letter, did he?"

"No," she said, almost as if he might have done.

"What's the party going to be?"

"With Adolphe, who can tell? By the way, it's in four days' time. On Monday. I'm leaving on Tuesday. In the morning. Why don't you leave then too? We could drive to the airport together. I love those Charles de Gaulle breakfasts with ancient rolls and uneatable jam. They are a sort of punishment for daring to leave France."

Anna was going on to a late supper. I walked alone to the Flore and sat between two silent couples and looked out, with them, at the indigo light above the glare of the streetlamps and the leaves on the trees beginning lightly, gently, to turn brown.

I sat and drank a brandy and thought of Richard. I realized with a shock that under all the talk and hesitation of the last two days I had really been thinking of nothing else. I found myself reliving the last evening Richard and I had spent together, two summers before.

Friends had lent me their house in Long Island for the weekend; Richard had left his then girlfriend in Boston to be with me (I was about to leave for Paris); we were sitting in the garden, drinking, the uncut grass around us scattered with bottles. It had been a calm evening. We had chosen our words with practiced care.

Then, suddenly, Richard brought his chair right in front of mine, so our knees touched. He leaned forward, and held my face between his hands, staring into my eyes. I could smell the warm champagne on his breath.

"What do you want me to do?" he said, closing his eyes. I was too startled to reply. It was the first time he had ever offered himself to me. I had long before given up hope of being lovers. He began to undo my shirt clumsily.

"What do you want me to do?" he repeated. He started to kiss me, to explore my mouth with his tongue. Then his body went dead. We carried on kissing but I felt shabby, and exhausted.

We got up, saying nothing, and went into the house to our separate rooms.

Later I went into his room.

"Will you sleep with me?" I asked him. "Not to make love. Just to sleep."

"No," he said gently.

I knelt down by his bed and hung my head.

"One day," he said, stroking my hair, "I will show you how much I love you."

He was crying.

When I awoke in the morning, he had left for New York.

In the four days after that evening in the Flore I bought my ticket to New York and sent a telegram to Mrs. Hughes, Richard's mother.

This is what I wrote in my diary, as if to Anna.

Adolphe said, "It was when you remembered the first meeting with Richard that you decided to go." Yes. Adolphe knew that there was something said then that had become a sort of pact between us.

Are all the threads in the first meeting? Is everything that happens afterwards an unraveling from that? Before I met Richard I had spent a year in India; I had decided to return to the West only temporarily, to take up a teaching post for six months in a university in North America (I was to lecture on Shakespearean tragedy). It was the first time I had ever been in the United States. I felt lonely and out of place.

The first meeting then . . .

I was sitting in a long dark oblong room behind a teak desk. There was nothing on the shadowed white walls and nothing else in the room but a canvas chair. The pupils who were going to take the class were coming in one by one to find out about it, to "suss me out." I was jittery at being in an American university for the first time, at being among a gaggle of semiotician colleagues with enormous salaries and fixed grim smiles. Each student face that came in seemed more depressing than the last, and blanker. My god, I said to myself, how will I talk about Hamlet to these faces, these checkered shirts, these dirty sneakers and Donald Duck watches?

Then, at the end of the afternoon, when the too-perfectly shaded lawn outside my window filled with Tai Chi fanatics, as I was packing up my books for the long glum walk back to my apartment on the other side of town, the door opened; Richard walked in. He was wearing black baggy pants and a turquoise sweater with patches at the elbows. He was five foot ten, with the lean angled body of a runner. His face caught the light from the lamp on my desk. I see it now—honey-colored, almost diaphanously clear-skinned, with two large, slightly unfocused, Chinese auburn eyes. It seemed more the face of an animal than of a young man. A deer or an Arctic fox.

I was twenty-six, he just twenty.

He walked in and started to smile. He put his books down, still smiling, a wary, scared smile, staring at me.

I found myself smiling back at him, leaning back in my chair to return his gaze. I arranged my right hand on the desk to give an impression of calm, of authority.

All I remember of what happened then are the words Adolphe somehow knows. Richard said, "I know nothing. I hardly know how to speak." I said, "I will teach you what I know. I will give you words."

This, Anna, after perhaps two minutes.

In those first words I hear all the fate of our love, all my temptation to power over him, all his temptation to give me a power I should not have had and he should not have wanted me to have, and would fear me for having.

You would say, Anna, "Your pathologies were suited! You love playing Prospero; you had found the ideal Caliban, one who looked like Ariel"—you would be right, but what marvels I saw by the light of pathology, what wonders! They were what I hated to give up, if I am honest, even more than him.

Going to find him now I must go with a clear heart, or there will be evil.

"I will teach you what I know. I will give you words." Did I not make some sort of promise to him then which I still, after all we have been through, have to fulfill?

Anna, it was Richard who first gave me the *I Ching* and taught me how to use it, and bought for me the three worn sallow Chinese coins that you love.

It's three on Sunday morning, the rough wall opposite is white and impassive in the moonlight, and I have just thrown the coins: hexagrams 6 and 43. "Conflict" and "Breakthrough."

From "Conflict": "The judge who must render the decision abides outside the dangerous situation. He can render a just decision only by remaining impartial."

From "Breakthrough": "Truthful announcement is fraught with danger. However, this danger leads to the light."

From "nine in the fourth place":

There is no skin on his thighs
And walking comes hard.

21

> If a man were to let himself be led like a sheep,
> Remorse would disappear.

> I sit in the white silence. I see Richard on that night in England when he went mad, staring at me, accusing me . . . Shall I ever make a good sheep?

Adolphe received us the next evening lying on his sofa with nothing on but a white kimono and a tiara, surrounded by nine burning candelabra.

"The tiara isn't real, you know, so you needn't look scandalized. I made love in it once in Las Vegas in Caesars Palace during an earthquake. Not a large earthquake. Just enough to shake the bed beautifully."

"I can see you're feeling well," said Anna, peeling off her black gloves.

"There's nothing like dying to make one feel marvelous," Adolphe said. "I saw my doctor today—the one with the platinum cufflinks. He has been wearing the officially dolorous expression recently and I asked him to cut it out. For one thing, it means I don't see his teeth, and I'm wild about his teeth. For another, he has one of those faces without thought which *cannot* look melancholy even if they try. I said I'd even pay him to smile, and then he *did* smile."

"How long did he give you?" asked Anna.

"That's what I love about you, darling. Your directness."

"You're the only person in the world I dare to be so direct with. How long?"

"Oh, quite a while." Adolphe smiled brilliantly.

"I'm worried you'll die while I'm away in India."

"I may, I well may. But why worry? I'll come back for years in your dreams and conversations. I know I'm unforgettable and so do you. So stop all this sentimental tripe. If I die tomorrow, I die tomorrow. *Finita, basta.* I'm not dressed like Rita Hayworth in *The Lady from Shanghai* to sit around making farewells."

We all stood for a moment, awkwardly.

"Well, Charlie boy, we're not very articulate this evening, are we? The soul full of trepidation, the heart in the balls, are they?"

"Don't be beastly."

"*That's* better . . . The good thing about you is that you can, momentarily, be gotten not to take yourself seriously. Cheer up, I know you're going into the labyrinth again and are scared to death of the Minotaur. Don't you see it is fear that gives the Minotaur its power? Just practice laughing at it and yourself, and you'll see that the huge slavering beast becomes a mouse. Remember that; remember me; and you'll be fine. More than that . . . but why should I tell you everything? Now that I'm about to disappear I mustn't get you *too* addicted to me."

"You're so odd these days, Adolphe."

"Curiouser and curiouser . . . You'll be staying with Antonia, presumably?"

"Off and on."

"Good luck. I'll write there. You write back."

"I promise."

"Well, on this our last evening for god only knows how long and for how many lifetimes—"

"Don't," said Anna.

"—I have some delights planned. But first we're going to Abdul the Prophet."

Anna and I stared at him.

"Abdul the what?" Anna said.

"Actually his name isn't Abdul. It's something Arabic

and quite unpronounceable. But I call him Abdul, and he doesn't seem to mind."

"The *prophet?*"

"He's not a prophet either. He's a ... a ... spider-lover. Yes, I suppose that is the most accurate description of him."

"Ugh!" said Anna. "I hate spiders."

"Will there be spiders there, at Abdul's?"

"Hundreds of them." Adolphe laughed.

"My god."

"Trust me. The chauffeur's waiting. You know how impatient Yugoslavs are."

Picking up his mink coat from the sofa, he flung it over his kimono, grabbed us both by the elbow, and with astonishing sudden strength swept us out of the room.

Leaning back against the squeaky gold leather of Adolphe's Silver Cloud, Anna said, "I had a pet canary called Abdul."

Adolphe looked straight ahead, adjusting his kimono under his mink.

"And this canary—"

"Shut up, Anna," said Adolphe. "Mock during or afterwards, but not before. One of Granny's only rules."

"I thought we were going to have a party, not an outing to a soothsayer who loves spiders."

"We *are* going to have a party. When have I ever failed you?"

"Never ask me questions like that." Anna laughed. "I have a memory as long as Luther's. Where *are* we going?"

"The rue de la Forge Royale."

"That crooked smelly little alley off Saint Antoine?"

"Yes, dear Anna. Full of fat Portuguese maids and dry cleaners that look as if they are gangsters' headquarters."

"The prophet lives *there?*"

"I offered years ago to buy him a place in the Sixième. He looked at me and said, 'But I love it here. The women in this street have real asses. What would I do with the anorexic asses of the rich?'"

"Oh, my god," groaned Anna. "A prophet who loves asses. I met quite enough of them in the sixties. Charles is being very silent."

"He's thinking of the Beloved," Adolphe said. "Of Andromeda across the ocean chained to her rock, waiting for Perseus."

"Wouldn't it be dreadful," Anna said, "if Perseus *was* the monster Andromeda was being sacrificed to?"

"Don't be oversubtle," Adolphe said. "It doesn't suit your looks. As for you, Charles, if you don't stop wearing that lugubrious expression, I'll make you do handstands up the stairs to Abdul's flat."

"Adolphe, Richard has *disappeared*. He might be dead."

"He is not dead. That I can assure you." Adolphe looked at both of us amusedly. "No, dear Charles, Andromeda is very much alive."

"Of course, you know everything."

"Not *everything*. Why do you writers always exaggerate?"

"We're there," Adolphe said.

We had arrived outside the battered khaki door of a large block of flats. The door opened and an Indian girl in a white sari stepped out. She was alone, young, with long dark braided hair. She looked at us for a moment, then walked on.

"Heavens," Anna said, "to have skin like that!"

"If Anna met the Virgin Mary," Adolphe said, "she would say, '*Who* designed those clothes?'"

"And *you* would ask for the telephone numbers of the seraphim flanking her."

Anna and Adolphe continued chattering and bickering through the door, into the dimly lit, smelly brown hall beyond it, and up the stairs.

"So what does this ass-loving prophet believe?" Anna was saying.

"Why don't you ask me?" a voice came from the next flight. "I might not tell you, of course. And then there are days I don't remember."

All the lights on the stairs went out.

"Stop it, Abdul," said Adolphe. "None of your tricks tonight."

"Who are you to talk?"

Laughter, loud and high-pitched. For a moment I had the distinct impression that there were several people laughing at once. Then Abdul's and Adolphe's voices merged. They were chanting something. I caught only the first line and the refrain.

> Death counting, counting, counting continually
> Does not count me.

Abdul was standing at the top of the stairs, in a pin-striped banker's suit. With his left arm around Adolphe. The lights went on. The chanting stopped.

"Damn," said Anna deliberately. "I've laddered my stocking."

With his right hand Abdul held before his face a large fan. He lowered it, and this podgy, blotchy face with round schoolboy glasses, very thick, peered down at us.

"Come in," Abdul boomed.

We were ushered into a vast room, at least thirty meters long, with dark green walls, filled with tapestries. The tapestries were all of spiders—purple spiders, blue spiders, elongated many-colored spiders, each calmly waiting at the center of an enormous web. Each tapestry had a black background; the webs differed in color. Some were red, some white, some a brilliant orange.

On the floor was a black silk carpet with a white sequinned web on it. Where the center of the web would have been there stood a statue of Kwannon, the Chinese Buddhist goddess of compassion.

I drew in my breath. It was exactly like the one I had often visited in the museum of the town where I first met Richard—the same height, about eight feet; the same material, a rich pink-and-green-painted terra cotta; and in the same position, with her hands outstretched in the *mudra* of protection. Only the headdress was different. In place of the usual crown, three crystal webs had been placed. A candle was lit in the middle of them; its refracted gold light played brokenly on the carpet.

The walls were lined with grandfather clocks of all kinds, each telling a different time. Curled up by the feet of the Kwannon was a thin ancient greyhound, with sad eyes, who stared at us.

"Where's Maya?" Adolphe asked.

"Maya's dead. She died last week in her sleep."

Adolphe turned to us. "Maya was Abdul's pet tarantula. She was humorous, too much so perhaps for this grim world."

Anna and I were both too dumfounded at the room,

at Abdul, at Adolphe's new world, to say anything. A room full of webs—commiseration over a dead tarantula—weird African chanting . . . all this was very far from our expectations of a last European evening.

I noticed with a start that Abdul had one blue eye and one green one. His hands were very long and thin. He came up to me and patted me on the head.

"Come and meet Sagesse."

At the mention of her name, the sad-eyed greyhound drew herself up and loped languidly across the room. I touched the dog's bony parchmentlike head.

"Sagesse will be with me until the end," Abdul said matter-of-factly, as if announcing the state of the weather.

"I need a Cointreau," Anna said.

Abdul pointed. "It is on the table to your left."

A small long thin glass table stood there with a glass of Cointreau on it. Beside it was a red rose.

"The rose is a present," Abdul said, "a compliment to beauty and courage."

"For a prophet, you are flattering."

"I am not a prophet," Abdul said. "I'm a charlatan with insights. Do you imagine a real prophet would need all this paraphernalia, this suit, these glasses, this greyhound? I'm shocked at you. And the red rose! A Ruritanian touch, wouldn't you say?"

Adolphe sat down by the Kwannon with the head of Sagesse cradled in his lap.

"I read," Anna said harshly, "about this experiment they did in California. They gave a lot of spiders different drugs—coke, hash, speed. The webs altered dramatically. Under speed, they had no order at all. Under hashish, they became concentric. Under coke, they became frantically tight."

"Which proves only," Abdul said, "that it is Conscious-ness that is the architect of the web."

Anna scowled and gulped her Cointreau.

"Anna darling," Adolphe said, "don't be aggressive. Abdul is rather excessive, I know, but surely you're used to that by now. And for a heterosexual he really is rather bright."

"I can't stand spiders. I can't stand prophets."

Abdul came up to Anna. "You must learn to forgive your mother."

"What the hell do you mean?"

"Remember her brooch? The one your father gave her for their fifth wedding anniversary? The spider . . ."

"Stop it."

Anna had put her hand up and covered her face. She was trembling.

Abdul continued: "It was the one she was wearing when she tried to strangle you."

Anna let out a short sharp scream. "I'm leaving."

I ran to her and held her.

Anna pulled herself together. "How do you know my mother had fits of madness? How—" She was unable to finish. "And how did you know about the brooch?"

Abdul rolled his eyes. "It is time I finished playing and we had something to drink! Anna, will you forgive me and take my hand?"

Abdul spoke with ancient courtesy.

"You are in great form, Abdul," Adolphe said admir-ingly. "Cancer suits you almost as much as it suits me."

"You flatter me."

Anna took Abdul's right hand and Adolphe took the other. He led them with me following to the sofa in the corner of the room.

"Adolphe and I," Abdul began, "have known each

other for a long time and in many times and places. I think of him as my wayward twin brother. He is frivolous and self-indulgent and vulgar, but he, as you know, understands many things."

"Don't be so bloody patronizing." Adolphe took Abdul's right hand and pretended to bite it.

"And of all the people he has known, Adolphe has selected you two to believe in most."

"God knows why," said Anna, still shaken.

Abdul went on. "As Adolphe intimated, I also am not well. You find me ill and tired. There are many things I would like to explain to you, many experiences I would like to share. We do not have the time now. Before long you both will understand much more than you do now."

"Even me?" Anna laughed, shrilly.

"Anna" (Abdul's voice was firm), "you underestimate yourself. It is a great mistake . . . Adolphe has brought you two here . . ."

"Why?" Anna asked, "Why *did* he bring us here?"

"We are all going on journeys. He wanted me to help you on yours."

Abdul looked towards the Kwannon in the center of the room. He turned to Anna. "There are many things I could tell you about your return to India, but it is essential for your sake that you do not know most of them. Ignorance is an essential ingredient in the first stages of experience."

"Thank you," Anna said. "Is there anything you *can* tell me?"

"Follow your dreams. Not your ideals, your dreams. You help others through them, but up to now you have not helped yourself. You must learn to!"

"What about Charles?" Anna asked.

"Ah, Charles." Abdul sighed.

I shivered.

"There is no need to be afraid," Abdul said, fixing on my face his astounding odd eyes.

"I am afraid."

"Of course. You have done a lot wrong. You have loved badly. The young man has loved badly. But—" He started to say something, but stopped himself. "No, no, let him find out for himself," he whispered. "It is much more helpful that way."

"Tell me something, at least."

"You are more receptive than Anna."

"More gullible," said Anna.

Abdul said, "Yes, I will tell you something." He closed his eyes.

"Not one of your trances, please," said Adolphe. "They can go on for hours, and we have another engagement. Please, Abdul."

"I'm not in trance, you idiot," came Abdul's voice, very loud and strong. "I see Richard clearly. In an empty room. He is alive."

"That much even I could have managed," said Anna.

"Yes, you could. You know a great deal already. Your dream was very revealing."

Anna whistled slowly.

"No," Abdul drawled, turning to me. "I have only one thing really to tell you. Remember the man you met years ago in a city of mosques."

I looked blank.

"I see the mosques," he went on, "but I have never been there, so I do not know the city. The man was thin and blond and he revealed something important to you which you have forgotten. You will remember it again when you need to."

"I certainly don't remember it now."

"No," he said. "You wouldn't."

I was beginning to feel angry. Abdul laughed.

"What children you are, both of you! First you test me and then you get riled because I won't give you everything!"

"Who was the Indian girl I saw coming out of the front door?" I asked suddenly.

"God knows," said Abdul, shrugging his shoulders. "This place is full of all sorts."

"Was she Indian?" Adolphe asked. "She looked Italian to me."

"She was wearing a sari, Adolphe."

"She was *not*. She was wearing a simple white suit."

"Pink," said Anna.

"We're losing our minds," I said.

"You have a long way to go yet," Abdul said. "A long way."

Anna stood up and asked the question I had been wanting to: "Why, Abdul, the webs?"

"Why, Abdul, the webs?" He repeated the question in an accurate mimicry of Anna's voice that startled us all. "Why the webs? They are there, that is all."

"Abdul, now don't be naughty," Adolphe said. "You've been so good so far."

"But Adolphe, they are so young," Abdul said.

"Give them a chance. They'll be as crazy as us at the end."

Abdul looked unconvinced and sulky.

"These things are impossible to put into words. And the symbols themselves are games, pointers, indications of a direction in which to travel and in no sense the journey itself."

"We know all that," said Adolphe. "Get to the point."

"Why don't you get to it if you're so wise?"

The sight of our two magi quarreling like schoolchildren made Anna and me smile.

"Why don't you speak in unison," Anna said, "Like people in a music-hall comedy act, and get it over with?"

To our astonishment, Adolphe turned to Abdul and said, "The long or the short version?"

"Oh, the short, I should think," said Abdul.

And they began:

> Death counting counting counting continually
>   does not count me
> Fire counting continually counting continually
>   does not count me
> Emptiness counting continually counting
>   counting does not count me
> The spider's web is round the corn-bin
> The spider's web is round the corn-bin.

After they had finished they stood up, bowed to each other like samurai, clapped hands, shook hands, and sat down.

"Any wiser?" they both asked.

"Not a bit," said Anna.

"Try this," said Adolphe, reciting slowly:

> Like a spider mounting
> on her web
> So from the soul
> issue all the worlds.

"Or this," Abdul boomed:

> In the old shrine
> Above the Buddha's head

The web
Shines in the full moon.

"Or this." Adolphe was singing now:

Maya tatam idam sarvam
By Me all this is woven.

"Now," said Abdul, mopping his brow, "we really must stop. Our friends will think we really have lost our marbles. Isn't that the English expression? Charles and Anna, let us begin at the beginning. You have heard, I think, of the word *tantra*."

"Abdul is such a pedant," Adolphe said.

"*Tantra* means threads. Threads as in weaving, or spinning. It is a perception of many cultures that all things, all being, the whole cosmos, are threaded together, as in a tapestry or carpet or web, inseparably eternally interrelated. Those disciplines that are called tantric are the ones designed to make the initiate aware of his relatedness to everything, aware of the eternal design and process at all times. This awareness is ecstasy and immortality."

"It's no good at all explaining." Adolphe sighed. "Anna and Charles will have to experience it, as we have. And they will."

"Don't be too sure," said Anna warily.

"Don't *you* be too sure," said Abdul.

I was in a daze and hungry for some explanation of *something*.

"Tell me," I asked, "why 'the spider's web is round the corn-bin'?"

"Adolphe and I were singing a Yoruba song," explained Abdul. "The Yoruba are an African tribe who live on corn. If the spider's web remains unbroken around the corn-bin, the corn has not been stolen and life will go on. The song itself is a kind of web of words and sounds, music and prayers, woven around the food of the tribe. And now, my children, I'm tired. You have your entertainments to go to . . . I'd like to say come again, but there will be no next time."

We did not know what to say, so shook hands and started to leave.

Anna turned at the door.

"The spider's web is round the bin."

"Corn-bin," Abdul corrected her, bowing.

We stood swaying slightly in the street for a moment before walking to the car. A light cold rain played on us. Every detail of the street seemed suddenly full of meaning—the stains the rain made on the wall opposite, the arrangement of the bits of torn newspaper in the gutter, the looks from the three Moroccan boys who passed us, at once come-hither and aloof, almost princely. Where the car was parked there was a tall birch sapling with many of its leaves still on it. Lit up in the mauve-gold light, it rustled in the wind. It seemed to be rustling for us, and at us.

As Adolphe got into the car, Anna recited: "The praying mantis devours its mate even while it is making love to him, the ceceris with a triple flash of its scimitar destroys the three centers of the buprestid's nervous system—"

"If you are trying to tell us," Adolphe interrupted, "that the insect world is not exactly a liberal paradise, I think we know that. The web itself can seem a net in which one is writhing . . . Of course. Don't be dull, my banana. Shiva dances and tramples, destroys and creates. What happens is far beyond all constructed morality, all pity. We have to be strong enough to see it plain. Guess what my favorite spider is, Charles."

"I'm not very up on spiders, Adolphe."

"Ah well, we all have faults."

"It'll probably be some wonderfully exotic one," I ventured, "with purple legs and a poison that makes all the limbs rot slowly, one by one."

"It is true," Adolphe said, "that I used to love the exotic varieties most. There is a kind in Mexico that can jump ten feet onto your shoulder. When I was filming with Hedy there, I used to threaten her with my pet one. 'If you don't turn up on time, I'll get my spider to jump on you.' Not even the jumping spider could save that film. Later, I had rather a banal period of flirting with the tarantula. Now I have chosen a humble Franciscan spider as my favorite, one that lives in the common fields of France and that has only one gift, but a beautiful one, one that I envy and try, in my poor way, to emulate."

"Adolphe, you are making us weep."

"If I could make you weep, my barracuda, the stars would fall from the sky and the moon rain Paco Rabanne. This gift is to change color, depending on what the spider is near. I call it 'ecstatic adaptation.' Not a bad phrase, eh? I should steal it, Charles. Yes, this spider changes color. When on a stone it is gray, when on grass it is green. And so it keeps safe and spins its harmless webs, which peasant women still use to bandage cuts with! No moist eyes yet?"

"It's as hard, Adolphe, to imagine you living a humble existence," Anna said, "as it is to imagine Marie Antoinette really milking cows."

36

"God," said Adolphe, "if I could only get my hands on *her* costumes! Think how that would annoy Marlene!"

"See what I mean?"

"Don't be superior and don't judge on externals. Sometimes they are just a screen, a sort of wonderful absurd smoke a self throws up to hide behind and get on with its real work."

"That can excuse anything."

"The girl is tough tonight. But then, she is always especially hard-nosed after she has been moved. True?"

"True," admitted Anna. "There was something moving about Abdul. How did you two meet?"

"A spider ran up my trousers in the Metro. I started to scream. He bent down and talked to it in a sort of wheedling kind tone and it came down."

"Rubbish."

"I was at the opera, in the front row. Sutherland was singing Lucia. Suddenly this spider started to crawl up her arms. She was in the most difficult part of the mad scene—"

"Rubbish."

"You are hard to please."

"I am like Pamina in *The Magic Flute*. Only the truth pleases me."

"Especially when it is six foot with muscles and perhaps a title. No, the real truth—how I love that phrase—of our meeting is, as you might expect, the strangest of all. I just sat next to him one day at the Deux Magots. He was reading a book on nuclear physics I had just finished—*The Dancing Wu Li Masters*. We found we had relativity and a certain taste in illuminated kitsch in common, and from there on became spiritual orgy-brothers. There's another phrase for you, Charles.

I hope you are listening and not just floating down the dark tides of memory."

"A lot of things seem to happen to you in the Deux Magots. Why don't you try the Closerie des Lilas for a change?"

"Your attempts at smartness, Charles, are like Anna's lunges at culture. Determined, but embarrassing. Anna, Charles is making a rather vulgar reference. About a day I was going to kill myself, and went for a last coffee at the DM. Actually, come to think of it, when I met Abdul I was sitting in the same place at almost the same time three years later. You do not have to look for the web. It emerges. Its long glistening lines suddenly shine up at you when you are not thinking about them at all."

The car came to a halt.

"Hop out, infants. We're there. It's just round the corner."

Neither Anna nor I had been watching where we were driving. We were in a small dark street, somewhere in the Marais.

Adolphe started to skip down the street in front of us, singing "Vissi d'alte" in falsetto, with all sorts of added sobs and arpeggios. For one frightening moment I thought he was going to do a handstand. He paused and seemed about to, but (thank god) thought better of it.

"Where does he get all that energy from?" Anna whispered.

"I asked him that recently and he replied, 'I get it from death. It's like in judo. You use the strength of your opponent against him.'"

Anna shivered. "A friend of mine, Claudio, died yesterday. The lover of Giovanni Borboni, the designer. From AIDS. He was thirty-three. One year older than you." Anna stopped. "How mysterious it is. Claudio dying yesterday, Adolphe dying but skipping down the street like Shirley Temple, you and I going off tomorrow . . . Are these connected?"

"Stop it, you two," Adolphe shouted at us from the end of the street. "Stop nattering. You're both so *mental.*" He was starting on the *Lucia* mad scene, as a threat.

"Don't die in India," I said to Anna.

"Strangely," Anna said, "I wouldn't mind dying in India. It's the one place I think I could die in without hysteria."

Adolphe bore down on us, singing. "Did I hear the word *dying?* Wash your mouths out with champagne!"

"Willingly," Anna said, "but where is it?"

"Just round the corner."

We turned the corner disbelievingly and there they were—three bottles of Moët Chandon, each in its individual icebucket, waiting for us.

"The spider's web, thank god," intoned Adolphe, "is also around the champagne. I forgot the glasses, but one can't think of everything at my age. Take up your buckets, and follow me."

From the left pocket of his mink he drew a long silver key. With the key, and muttering some words I couldn't hear, Adolphe opened a small iron gate to the left of the buckets.

"Enter," he said, popping the cork of the first bottle loudly into the night. "Come into the center of the web of Paris."

"If anyone says the word *web* again . . ." said Anna, and then stopped. She looked around. "Adolphe, this is really too much."

"Too much for whom?" Adolphe asked smugly. "Don't

39

stand there like extras from *Spartacus*. Come in. Romp and revel. Leave your minds at the door."

We were in a small moonlit square, flanked on all sides by tall dark walls.

"Look at the name, darling," Adolphe whispered, pointing to a small sign. "The place Georges Cain! Isn't that perfect? Was that straggly grass over there fed with Abel's blood? It might have been. Anything might have happened here. Look around. Drink in the madness of it."

Anna and I stood, silent and astonished. Roman sarcophagi lay in the grass, yawning in decay; a tall pillar with its capital wreathed in ivy stood to our left; masks grinned at us from the walls, masks of satyrs, of ancient philosophers made absurd by the festoons of moonlit creeper hanging from their ears. A vast portico was fixed into the wall to our right, its white fluted columns darkened by the Parisian night and muffled by plants that writhed around it in tropical abandon. In the midst of it there were two nymphs, their marble skirts flying in an imaginary wind, holding up an oval in which there had once been a bust (we could see its stand) but now was only the flickering moonlight.

"To think that you have seen nothing yet," said Adolphe, rubbing his hands like a magician in a pantomime.

"It's wonderfully creepy," said Anna. "It's a graveyard of all the fantasies of Paris. Rome and Greece end here, Mansart and Racine . . ."

"My god, she's got it badly," said Adolphe. "That's good. Have another swig of the champers. You'll never know what you might see."

"None of this is real, is it?" I said to Adolphe. "You had it put up this afternoon."

40

"Could even I have got the creepers to grow like that? Look into the sarcophagi—they each have their variety of livid viridian moss. Where could I have bought that? And the lizards! Tiny ones, fat ones . . . They're sleeping now, but you should see them by sunlight. I think they come from all over France to be here. They probably swim the Atlantic to be here, or hide in the fuselage of Concorde."

Anna turned away.

"Spiders and lizards . . . Oh lord, Adolphe, why did you never warn me about *these* perversions of yours?"

"Lizards are very dumb compared to spiders. But I like the way they breathe. They resurrect themselves at each breath."

Anna bumped against something and shrieked.

"Oh, but it's beautiful," she said, bending down.

The sculptured face of a young woman stared up at us from the grass. She had wide sun-drunken eyes, like those of the Cycladic mother-goddesses, and a smile like theirs, subtle and delicate as if the lips had been parted by a wind.

"Ah, there is beauty in the desolation," said Adolphe in his "German" voice. "And we are never knowing when we will find it."

Anna stroked the statue's cheeks.

"You're drunk," I said.

Adolphe stood apart with an odd smile on his face. "And now, my children . . . look around *really*. What do you see?"

"What are we supposed to see?"

"Oh pondsnipe, when will you learn to trust your own madness and not borrow mine?"

We stood, gazing at the walls, the sarcophagi, the pillar with its head of ivy, the portico . . .

"I see the clock above the portico," I said. "It's got only one hand and it has stopped at midnight."

Anna giggled. "That is good. At *midnight!* 'And we,'" she intoned, "'are climbing towards midnight.' Georg Trakl."

"Some of us," Adolphe said, "are already there."

"The whole world is there," I said, drunk.

"Go on in that vein, pondy. I like it best when you are apocalyptic."

"This is the midnight garden, isn't it? The place where everything dissolves."

"That's enough; look harder." Adolphe went over to the wall near the portico, spread his arms, and leaned against it. Above him grinned the mask of a Silenus.

The grasses rustled. Anna started.

"Don't worry," said Adolphe. "It's just Prajna."

A huge sleek cat emerged from the night and nuzzled against Adolphe's legs. It had a jet-black body and a white face with fierce eyes. Its purr seemed to fill the garden.

"It's not a cat. It's a dinosaur," Anna said.

"Cocteau wrote a poem to it on one of our evenings here. 'O ruin-haunting cat with eyes that see beyond destruction, guide us . . . ' Where? I've forgotten. It's a rotten poem."

"But Cocteau died—"

"It's a very old cat," Adolphe said solemnly. "Look about you. What do you *see?* I'm not going to do everything for you. Yes, I am, but I want you to show a *little* willing! Walk around. Kneel. Sing songs. You'll get it if you look for it, as Saint Francis said, or should have."

"More like the Rolling Stones than Saint Francis," Anna said.

Prajna gave a growl.

42

"You see, Anna," Adolphe said with a laugh, "the gods are judging you."

Anna knelt and started calling to the cat. "Come here, you stegosaurus. Help me. Adolphe is testing me and I'm plastered and I need all the help I can get." The cat gave a great yawn and came over to where she was kneeling.

I was walking round the square, peering into the shadowy corners, trying to guess what Adolphe wanted us to see. There was a graffito on the wall near the portico: GLORIA MUNDI, crossed out in red and changed to GLORIA MUNDORUM. "Glory of the world," changed to "Glory of the worlds" . . . How many worlds are there, I thought, how many worlds are there even here where I stand, swaying slightly. I remembered a soft-voiced physicist in Oxford explaining to me patiently his theory of sheets: "Peel the sheets, my boy . . . a thousand sheets, a thousand dimensions in every megasecond." My mind went white. Too much champagne, too much everything. I suddenly thought of Richard and wished he were here with us. *He* would see what I could not. I longed to be aware, to be visionary. Richard was visionary . . .

I shook. How had I forgotten that whole part of him? It was what I had loved most. And to remember it here, staring at this wall . . . I saw his face as I had once seen it when I had walked into his room. He had been sitting looking out of the window, at the sun on the grass. When he turned to me, his eyes were sunken and very distant.

Suddenly Adolphe was standing by me. "Earth to pondsnipe. Come in, pondy."

"Remembering Richard."

"Ah, what a title! Don't lose that one!"

Anna called out behind us. "Hey, you two, I've got it.

43

I've finally got it. Thought you had us, didn't you Adolphe? Well, come here." She was summoning us, in triumph. The cat was now sitting on her shoulder.

Anna looked almost august, there in the moonlight with the cat. She had kicked off her shoes, though, and was standing on a little pile of crisp fallen leaves. "Charles," she said, "come here."

Suddenly Adolphe shrieked, "Charles, you beast! You monster! You're wearing *Giorgio!* I told you to wash that filthy stuff off. Only Warren Beatty should wear rubbish like that. It's Guerlain or else Le Bal de Monsieur or A Bas Monsieur!"

"We're standing on the edge of revelation and you talk about aftershave. Shame on you."

"Shame on yourself. All beauty is connected. The web of loveliness does not contain Giorgio—I assure you!"

Anna was ignoring us both, staring out at the square.

"Shut up. Listen. You, of course, Adolphe, know what I am going to say. The square is made of two webs; it is a mandala. The two inner webs are surrounded by the debris we see around us—the wreckage." She said *wreckage* with a long roll on the *r*. "It is as if to get to the first web—on which we are standing—you have to have seen the wreckage, realized it, understood and suffered it, gazed thoroughly at all the broken pillars and ruined porticoes of your life."

"Very poetic," said Adolphe. "Trakl?"

"Be quiet. We are, as I said, standing on the first of the two webs. It is covered with fallen leaves."

"It would be. It's autumn."

"Adolphe, please. You're just jealous that I understood. This web is the web of memory, of meditation, that suffers time and the changes of the ego . . . And in the middle over there, down the stone steps . . ."

44

I had not seen the small stone steps leading down into a central circle.

"And in the middle down there," Anna repeated, "is the central web. Do you see what I see?"

I had been so fascinated by the walls and the sarcophagi that I had not thought to look at the middle of the square.

"Move closer."

"Did you and Adolphe arrange all this beforehand just to make me look dumb?"

"Don't be vain. Look at it."

"It is unbelievably bad," I said, in revenge.

"Yes, but what is it of?"

"Flora and her chariot," Adolphe interrupted, "by Laurent Magnier. Eighteenth century. Rococo. Spring with the wind about her body, rising from her bed of mother-of-pearl, the new breath, the new world."

"It's mad," I said. "It's camp."

"It's at the center of the world," Anna said. "A young girl bringing in a new world."

Adolphe looked at her. "Well done."

"Whenever you congratulate me I feel like hitting you."

"Do. Remember I'm not a gentleman and so will hit you back . . . Anna has guessed right. The square is a mandala, made of two webs. There is one last thing that I have to show you."

"You *would* keep it for yourself," said Anna.

"Magicians must be allowed their tricks, don't you think? Humor me. You do not have the Bride among you long."

We followed him across the square to its far right-hand corner.

"Close your eyes," Adolphe ordered.

45

"This is like Girl Guide camp," Anna said.

"Open."

Before us, pinned to the wall, was a large rosette of stone. From a tangle of stone leaves in the middle was raised a small mandala. In this there was the beautiful naked figure of a young woman with long braided hair. Over the entire surface of the rosette there were spiders' webs, hundreds of them; only the central mandala with the body of the woman was free of their intricate dazzle. Adolphe went over to the stone woman and touched her hair. Then he came over to us and touched both our foreheads lightly.

"Don't look so *serious!* It's *fun!*"

Prajna had appeared out of the dark and sprung into Adolphe's arms. "Well, my darlings," he said quietly, "it is time to go. I have shown you what I can, what I know. It isn't very much. I belong to the outside of the mandala, the debris, the porticoes, the clock stopped at midnight. I do a damn good job of belonging there, I must say . . . You two will travel further, far beyond the square Cain. Won't they, Prajna? Little do they know what an adventure they are on. Look at them. Not at first sight a very appetizing pair, would you say? But decent, for all that, and worth some of the money and love I have lavished on them. No more Giorgio, Charles. Write to me every day. I want to know all. And you, Anna, you rat . . . well, at least I cured you of Opium. Remember the fights we had over that? You write to Charles and me constantly. What's the use of living in this rotten old world if one can't at least use its services? We will be strongly, extraordinarily, *in touch,* thanks to God and the *poste restante.* I will lecture you both in your dreams."

"Don't you *dare*," said Anna.

Prajna jumped out of Adolph's arms and ran off into the moonlit grass.

That night I dreamt of Richard.

It was a summer afternoon. He and I were sitting in deck chairs in the place Georges Cain by the statue of Flora and the red roses that clustered thickly round its base.

Richard was tanned and shirtless. A pile of letters stood by his chair—the letters he had written me over the years—and he was reading them, laughing.

"'I have tortured your soul, I know.'

"'I do not want to be your lover. I want to be your Siamese twin.'

"'Do not wait for me; it would be suicide, and murder.'"

Suddenly, we were both laughing. Richard reached into his shorts, found a lighter, and lit the pile of letters. We watched them burn.

Richard stood up. He came over to me and knelt by the side of my chair. His warm acrid smell swept over me. I closed my eyes.

"Can't you see?" he whispered. "Can't you see I'm ready?"

When I opened my eyes, I was sitting up in bed in Paris staring across at the cracked white wall. In the courtyard below, the concierge was screaming at her dog.

·TWO·

CHARLES TO ADOLPHE

New York

Adolphe, I miss you already. How dare you be so in-
dispensable? I thought of writing this in my Sanskrit
script, to make you really suffer, but pity for your tired
old eyes intervened (you, whose eyes are about as tired
as Lucille Ball's). So here I am typing long past midnight
on Antonia's antique typewriter. In between sentences I
get up and wander round the Great She's apartment,
stumbling with jet lag and munching down a pile of ham
sandwiches. Antonia herself is not here. Thank god. In
my current rickety state I don't relish days of heavy
Freudian conversation on nothing but diet bread, Swiss
cheese, and the occasional wrinkled black olive. She is
on a lake in Minnesota doing exercises with Lily, bored
out of her skull but bravely deciding to stick it out for
another two weeks.

Before I tell you what is really going on, I mean,
GOING ON (heavy sighs and reachings for the vodka
bottle), I want to say that I am furious about you and
the web thing. Oh, not for any grand reason, and not
because I have anything philosophically, spiritually, erot-
ically, or dietically against it, but because now—may all
your Callas records be broken one by one—I see them

everywhere. I saw them in the palms of the customs official at Kennedy. I saw them in the strands of the rain falling on the taxi as we went over the bridge. Tomorrow I will be seeing them in curls on the subway, book jackets, bagels . . . See what you have done to me! The good thing is that although I say I miss you (I do!), I feel the threads between us are indissoluble, that if I pull at my end, I can feel you from your eyrie across the Atlantic pulling back.

You've noticed, I know, how silent I've been since The Letter—I think I'm beginning to understand why.

I've lit six candles for you under Antonia's terra-cotta Kali. Kali's red tongue is waggling at me through the dark. Looks as if Antonia had just dipped it in blood.

Start, Charles, start, or you'll never start.

I am going to get to the point, Adolphe. I just need a little courage.

Sitting in the plane I made a note of my various fears.

Fear One: That Richard will be stir-crazy when and if I ever find him. And full of hatred.

Fear Two: Related to the above. That the hatred will be articulate, and accurate enough to be deadly.

Fear Three: That I will hate him if he hurts me too much, dump him or savage him, and drive him further over the edge . . .

These are the Fears Melodramatic (and, naturally, the ones I entertain most).

Fear Four: That I will be of no use. That all this worry, time, expense, dredging up of the past, will be useless.

Fear Five: Related to the above. That he couldn't care less whether I lived or died, and so when and if I find him, he will stare at me with half-closed eyes and say, "Who paid you to come? Get back to your life in Paris

or wherever the hell you are sashaying about now."
"Sashaying" is not Richard's kind of word—he's too
wasp—but his hands and eyes would say something like
it. I'm vain enough to prefer to be demonic rather than
dull.

Then there is the overarching fear of him, of what we
were, of the past, eating into, accusing, deriding the
present, making it flat and uninhabitable.

And you? You kept making mysterious promises to
tell me everything. If you don't I'll . . . I'll . . . I'll do such
things as make Kali's tongue gleam even more redly.

Anna will be in Delhi by now. Lucky her.

Charles

ADOLPHE TO CHARLES

Paris

Pondsnipe—

Wash your socks.
Get enough sleep.
Eat wholewheat bread and drink fresh-crushed orange
juice.

Adolphe

CHARLES TO ADOLPHE

I just posted the first letter.
I can't sleep and I feel so lagged I'm hallucinating.
Let me go on about Richard. Turn Callas up loud if
this bores you.

Some loves are purely, deeply physical. I did love Richard physically—his arms, the honeyed fuzz above his bellybutton, all that—but always with a fear, a reluctance, that derived from a deeper love, a psychic passion.

The dreams. One in particular I remember yesterday. I had it several times and *he* had it several times, in variations of course . . .

We were always in a tropical landscape, he and I, together—alone—sometimes by a river, sometimes on the steps of a ghat leading up from the water, once in the forecourt of an old temple. We would be sitting, looking at each other. It was as if, as well as seeing our own vision, we saw also what the other saw. I would look at him and his face would change—I would see the face of a bird or a fox or an old woman or sometimes just the sky filled with lightly burning cloud. He would look into my face and see forests, rivers, most often the bottom of the sea and the transparent fishes he loves. There was never fear in any of these apparitions. They filled us both with wonder.

In those days before the "madness" Richard would often have fits. That is the word he used for them. Fits in which he would suddenly feel each cell of himself agonizingly detach itself from the others and start to scream in separation (he said he felt as if he were being stretched in pain over the whole sky). He said that I was the first person he had ever told, that he had had them since childhood but had never before believed in anyone enough to tell him about them.

How bad he looked, Adolphe, when he came out of them—pale, wrung out, his dark eyes sunken in rings of black. He hardly seemed alive. He said that the only

54

thing that saved him in the fits was the repetition of my name. He would repeat it endlessly (he said) without drawing breath, and after each repetition, "He loves me," "He loves me." It was frightening, feeling that only my love saved him from chaos—and flattering, of course. I see now that he may well have wanted to make me powerless by giving me a position so exalted that it prevented anything else from happening. The savior could not become the lover . . .

Still, I failed him. This is what is hard to remember. I failed him by desiring him. He was in love with me but he was terrified of sex. Once he described to me how at the age of four he heard his parents making love. He knew it was ridiculous, the amount of emotion he felt— at his mother's screams, his father's slow savage grunts (his words, I remember them). He knew consciously that many people have that first shock. But in his case, his parents divorced when he was eight—bloodily, melo-dramatically—leaving him with his mother to watch her drink, become promiscuous, hate herself as she aged.

Oh god, I can hear you saying, an old story, *eine alte Geschichte*. Yes, but he was tender, Adolphe, a sort of lost child when I met him, and he was then twenty. What can he have been like as a real child? I hardly dare imagine his vulnerability. How could he believe in physical love after he had seen what it had done to his mother? How could he believe in his manhood when he had seen his father—whom he loved—destroy not only his mother but a succession of "stepmothers" by his sexual careless-ness? How could he after that face that the person he loved most was not the kind of angelic rich blonde girl he was expected to have loved but a *man*, an odd English aesthete at that?

55

I should have understood all this. I should have been brave enough to give without asking for anything . . . How easy to say that now, sitting here in Antonia's flat writing to you and attempting to make sense (terrible phrase) of it all. I should have, but I could not. I was too hungry, too much in love, too in love with love. But I was old enough to know what not to do, what not to ask. And I still did what I wanted to and asked what I wanted. That was my guilt, Adolphe, one of them, the chief of them.

And the sadness of this is, we did live at moments a true, clear love. It was in the joy we knew when we walked together in the autumn woods of that North American town; it was in the candor with which we laid bare our lives to each other; it was in the calm of the long hours listening to music together or visiting the museum or reading. How could I destroy this love?

Charles

ADOLPHE TO CHARLES

Dear Buffeted Pondy

Don't enjoy your suffering *too* much, although I don't see why you shouldn't have a bit of a good time with it.

All part of the warp and woof, old bean. I'm not being heartless (I am!), but I want you to remember four things.

ONE [in red and in capitals]

GUILT CAN BE ANOTHER VANITY AS YOU SAY AND ONE CAN NEVER SAY IT ENOUGH.

56

THE GAME AND DANCE ARE NOT YET OVER AND YOU HAVE NO IDEA WHERE THEY ARE GOING. DON'T DIVE INTO FINAL MOURNING JUST YET, HOWEVER GREAT YOU LOOK IN BLACK.

TWO

He may have needed to break, this Richard-egg. What would he have been had he not met you? Another American neurotic, with a spoiled childhood and a rather overhealthy bank account. Summers on the Cape, a job in publishing. He gave *you* the visions, the whatnot, the whole shebang. You gave *him* the visions, the whatnot, too.

THREE

I'm not sure what to say here except go on taking the fruit juice and getting enough sleep and keeping your chin up.

FOUR

I don't believe for a second all this stuff about your wicked wretched ego wanting to drag him into bed and he being above it all. I like it; it has a wild ring; but I don't believe it. Why can't one have eternity *and* sex? Sex is the tango of eternity on this earth and there is no reason why people should not taste in abandon something of the joys of God himself. Put that in your pipe and smoke it. And put it in *his* pipe too if you get the chance. Oh Adolphe, such filth. No, pondsnipe, you were *both* neurotic, afraid of sex, the whole thing, and you rationalized that fear and indulged it. Not that your visions weren't real and beautiful—but they were partial. *There are others.*

My optimism must seem frivolous to you in your *frater dolorosus* phase, with stigmata all over you like measles.

57

But then I am nine hundred years old and totally de-voted to having the BEST POSSIBLE TIME.

Don't be inhibited by all this wisdom from going on pouring it all out. It's much more fun than reading the newspapers.

Adolphe

P.S. I want you to know that I am going through the most exciting period of my life. I shall pour it on you when I understand it more.

P.P.S. *Never* be abashed about your visions. Only bores, Freudians, and Englishmen don't trust their visions. Think of ancient Egypt, India, China, medieval Europe, Rumi, Eckhart, Shankara, and the Buddha, and take heart and go on having as many visions as you damn well please. They are legal after all. Only keep your sense of humor *intact*.

Not a word from Anna. But then Indian posts are slower even than Bergman films.

CHARLES TO ADOLPHE

New York

Adolphe—

Thanks for the knocks on the head. I've slept, thought, walked round and round Central Park in the sharp cold sun, and feel a lot saner.

I thought I saw you in the street yesterday. I was coming out of the coffee shop on Seventy-fifth and Madison—the one with the vast waitress with black teeth—and there you were, just romping round the corner out of sight. The spitting image of you, at least from the back. Purple cap, purple caftan, your arms . . . I ran after "you," but clearly "you" had gone in somewhere. You aren't tracking me, are you? Or do you have the yogic powers of displacement? I read about them once and envied the people who developed them *like crazy.* Fancy being able to have nine lives at once. One writing letters, one making love to Puerto Ricans, one reading the collected works of Balzac. Etc. I revere you but I don't think you're that far developed. Anyway, it was very odd. I was elated at seeing you, though. Made me feel myself again.

I've been waiting to hear from Mrs. Hughes. Naturally I cabled her before I left, sending her Antonia's address and telephone number, and asking her to ring me as soon as possible. Not a word. I'm relieved. It gives me some breathing space, some more time, and as you must have seen from my first two letters I badly need time, to get myself "straight" before whatever happens.

Something even stranger than seeing you happened later on in the day. I remember us once a few years ago having a discussion about the objects people collect around them and how they reveal their personality. You said, "If you want to stay in contact with someone, hold or be close to one of the objects they love." You went on and on about how you'd been told this by an African ju-ju man, and how you'd done it for years as a way of entering the field of the one you loved, of becoming sensitive to whatever signals they were emitting from wherever they were. I didn't really understand at the time, and I thought you were performing Yourself with your customary brio.

Well, I have brought to New York some of the objects

that Richard gave me or that I found after his visits. I have a photograph of Einstein he sent me after a quarrel (Richard loved his gentle face and electromagnetic hair). I have one of Richard's running jerseys (don't smile). I hid it when he came to see me one afternoon; it smelt of him for a long time and I've never cleaned it. It is here on my desk as I write—green, with white stripes, shrunken now, so it seems it could fit a child. During the night I was writing you these letters—to feel him close, to *hear* him—I was playing on Antonia's gramophone the music he loves—Vivaldi's flute concerti, the *Four Seasons*. Listening to the expansive and almost naive joy of Vivaldi made me feel Richard's purity acutely (and also my impatience with it). Yesterday morning, when I awoke after the night of writing to you and listening to "his" music, I felt Richard all about me. I felt as I almost always felt when I was near him, stripped and raw.

I walked over to the Metropolitan to look at paintings we had studied together. Of all painters, it is Rembrandt that Richard loves most, the early Rembrandt especially. I have here a letter of his written a year ago: in it he talks of the early wedding portraits of the man and his wife that hang in the same room as *Aristotle Contemplating the Bust of Homer.*

> Remember the double wedding portraits of the man and his wife, which I told you I loved, but you said you didn't like as much as the others? They still hit me head on with their black black clothes and white white ruffs against their luminous background. The woman's eyes are wise, caught in a bourgeois body and shadowed by a cowed vulnerable forehead; her hands glow, as does her face, and if you stand back the hands and face emerge like glowing stars in the black night of her dress. There

is a soft crescent-shaped shadow that circles her neck on the platform of the white ruff. Pearls sparkle at the base of her neck near the ruff, but then disappear into shadow as they move around to the dark side.

I had been aware when I first read that description that Richard was, whether consciously or not, describing something in his own psyche, as well as Rembrandt's painting. So I went yesterday morning to sit in front of the painting, read the letter over, and be with him. I must be with Richard, I felt, at his best, in order to release both of us from whatever rancor or fear I still feel, in order to—and how to explain this?—to purify the path to whatever is going to happen.

I sat in the room with the painting for about an hour. I felt I was beginning to see it with his eyes, to see the hands and face "like glowing stars," to feel the depth of his sympathy for that scared young woman. Richard loves "ordinary" things—he would often stop me in the street to point out the way a dog was walking or the face of an old man bent over his coffee in a diner. The rooms he lived in, like the clothes he wore, were always simple, uncluttered.

Richard had a botany teacher—a man—when he was about fourteen, who remained a sort of model for him. This teacher used to take his class on long walks through the woods and invite them to listen to the sounds of the animals and birds. He knew each sound by heart and would explain the music of the woods to them, whole life-stories from one sound. Richard would often— sometimes angrily—chide or mock me for what he saw as my "unnaturalness," my exaggeration. And I would defend myself by calling him sentimental, American, too self-effacing, accusing him of hiding from greatness in a sort of shy private underworld, a fantasy of natural-ness which was really only a substitute for childhood. Which was partly true of course.

Sitting there, however, for that hour, in front of "his" painting, I felt again, very strongly, Richard's clear spirit. I saw Richard's face six years ago in the face of the Rembrandt wife, Richard's hands behind her hands. I felt closer to him than I had for years.

I was about to leave the room when Susan walked in. Susan, of all people. You do not know who Susan is. I can't help feeling you are lucky not to know Susan, al-though no doubt you have had your Susans. Remember telling me once about that countess you found in bed at least five times with different lovers of yours? And how you could never understand what they found in her? So far Susan has cropped up twice in my life with two dif-ferent men, years and continents apart. The second was with that *louche* Canadian last summer you warned me about (remember him? Trying to be a poet in a garret and actually living off Papa). Susan—then in Paris to do a thesis on Benjamin—was "seeing" him. The first was Richard. In the first three months of our friendship, Richard was using her and she was using him in that no-nonsense, no-romance, sex-for-kicks-and-health way that American college students have perfected. Richard needed her more probably to "prove" that he was straight. Whatever the reason, it hurt. And here she was, Susan, with her close-cropped boyish blonde hair, her shrewd unsparkling green eyes, her green silk blouse, white Italian sweater, and obligatory tights and white sneakers. Carrying Benjamin's *Illuminations*. She was thinner than last summer, I noted with chagrin, thinner, more elegant. Paris and the "poet" had been good for her.

Me: Still working on Benjamin, I see.

Susan: It's a complicated subject.

Me: He wrote such difficult German.

Susan: I'm not sure it is that difficult.

We stood awkwardly; and then I said, "We must talk properly. I'm here because of Richard. His mother wrote to me that he has disappeared. I'm trying to find him." I must have said it very wildly, because she gave me one of her long-suffering Yankee looks. But she said "Okay" in her usual flat, unenthusiastic way.

Lunch with Susan. I was shaking a little from the shock of having met her, on *that* day and in *that* place (I didn't tell her about the painting, I didn't want to share that intimate revelation of Richard with her). We talked, after the first half-pleasantries, almost exclusively about Richard and about that time six years ago. I plied her with cocktails, and she became less guarded.

Me: Did you love Richard?

Susan: No. I found him sexy. I liked his flute-playing. I liked that dreamy look he had when he looked at you and thought you didn't notice — a sort of accepting look. I liked his hands. I didn't love him because I was afraid to.

Me: Why afraid?

Susan: Weren't *you* afraid? I mean — he was so raw. It was like loving a baby mouse or a cat with three legs. I admired you for loving him. No, that's not true. That's the gin talking . . . I thought you were a fool. I didn't really see what you saw in him. If you were after American chicken — excuse me — there were lots of prettier, less screwed-up ones around. The place was crawling with them, in their jumpsuits and short hair. But you were after drama, tragedy. I could tell. You got it.

(Pause.)

63

I suppose I was jealous of your love for him. You were so intense together. I mean, any room the two of you were in was like clam chowder—thick, *thick.* The silences! The looks! It bored and scared me. And it scared him. You know how it scared him. He used to say, "Doesn't Charles ever relax?" As if *he* ever relaxed. He would ask me, "Do you think I'm bisexual?" when it was obvious, and one of the good things about him. I like the more feminine kind of man.

At least we had the grace to grin at each other at that moment. Not a friendly grin exactly; the way leopards might grin at each other in the jungle.

Me: Where do you think he is?

Susan: He's probably found some nice Jewish girl from Queens to make soup for him and not ask too much. I don't know. One thing I can tell you, though. He's not dead.

Me: How do you know for certain?

Susan smiled in triumph. "I spoke to him last week. He usually writes around my birthday or at Christmas. It was my birthday last week and he rang. I didn't know he was 'missing' and so I didn't ask him where he was. I assumed he was *chez lui.*"

Me (keeping my voice calm): What did he say he was doing?

Susan: You know Richard. Loves being mysterious. I think he said he was writing something. But then he always says he's writing or painting something. Most of the time he's doing nothing, dreaming, jogging round the woods, taking odd jobs, working in bars, scrounging off his parents. You know the kind of upper-class American bum thing. He's great at it. I think he said he was okay. I'm not sure. Anyway, it was good to hear from

64

him. His voice sounded good on the phone. I wish I could tell you more. I could invent something else if you wanted. If *that* would make you happy. (Pause.) I tell you one thing. I never believed he was that crazy. I knew he was screwed up. But crazy, *really* crazy, no. I think he was taking time off. Don't ask me for what. I'm not sure. And I don't think Richard is the sort to kill himself.

Me: And do you know anyone who is?

Susan (slowly and very coolly): Yes. Me. I've tried four times.

Me: You're lying.

Susan: Yes, but I had you fooled for a second, didn't I? I know how you've always despised me, thought me vulgar, grabby. I am vulgar. I am grabby. I want to have a good time.

Susan stood up, straightened her hair (already very straight) in the mirror, and then said, "Oh, yes, one thing. Richard did say he'd read your new book. The one that takes place in Venice."

"Paris."

"Paris. He liked it."

"Thank you."

"Good luck. Say hello to Richard from me when you see him."

She kissed me, as Paris had trained her how to, three times on the cheek.

So he is alive, Adolphe. He is *alive.* You bastard, you were right. I don't mean "you bastard," I mean "hooray." And something in Susan's flat way of telling everything reassured me mysteriously. We shall see.

Just this minute Mrs. Hughes left a message on Antonia's answering machine. A warm nervous voice. Eerily like Richard's. "I hope you will be able to make lunch at

65

the Veau d'Or tomorrow." I rang back and left a message on *her* answering machine. From machine to machine . . . The Veau d'Or, Adolphe, was where Richard and I always ate in New York, even when we couldn't afford it, because he loved the mirrors and the old waiter at the cocktail bar with his white moustache. To meet his mother in the body of the Golden Calf. Richard must be smiling to himself somewhere.

Adolphe—I'm self-absorbed at the moment, I know, but tell me what is going on with you. What is this exciting new thing? You are always with me under all the other things. You'll only half believe me, I know, but it hurts me to be away from you at this time, when there is so little time. And yet you are here.

Charles

ADOLPHE TO CHARLES

Paris

Pondy—How perfect that she should be called Susan. Mine were always called Catherine and had pointed little features and stainless-steel smiles. In most cases, of course, they did me a favor in taking off my hands the young shit of the moment. I wept and fell down stairs and clutched absinthe bottles, enjoying every second of it, but usually after three months (when Ambivalent had already moved on to Giorgio or Vivienne or Brazil) I found that I was a lot happier and more myself without him—and a lot richer too. Susan did after all do you the great favor of getting rid of that Canadian of last summer (whose name we will not mention), whom you had

66

set up as your usual mixture of Antinois, Rimbaud, and the young Lord Krishna, but who was in fact (as anyone could see) a coked-out spiritual coprophile from the suburbs of Alberta who would have eaten you alive, and without cutlery.

Now, quite enough about you. For *my* news. Just because I'm cooped up in bed all day, it doesn't mean I have nothing to do but scribble to you and ramble over my memories like Pauline Bonaparte. I'm not interested in the past. It's the future that electrifies me, banana.

I'm keeping the really juicy bit until last, by the way, so you'll have to read to the end.

First—dolphins. In a way they *do* come first. Abdul met a man who knew the man who knew *the* dolphin man, and this man came into my boudoir—he's a very slow-speaking American who couldn't tell a lie even if the future of mankind depended on it—sat gingerly in green corduroy on the edge of my bed, and talked about dolphins. I was so interested I even managed to concentrate and not interrupt, although I was dying to tell him the story of Elsa Maxwell and the dolphin off Crete. Looking back, I'm rather glad I didn't. I think he's *serious,* darling.

Well, after telling me what everyone knows about them, he then began—I did give him champagne cocktails, and I do as you know have a way of *extracting* things from people—he started to tell me how he would talk to his dolphin when the dolphin wasn't there, I mean miles away at sea. I got very interested. "What do you talk about? Reaganomics? The latest discoveries in astrophysics?" He looked at me patiently. "No," he said. "I tell him that I miss him and that I will meet him, say, eight miles away at the edge of the Cape." I almost called

Abdul then and there to whisper in our code, "Come and get this madman out of my boudoir," for I am frail, on the edge of the abyss, etc., and what if he did get *really* loopy? But looking at him, at his spectacles, at the patches on his trousers, at his Yankee good-as-bread face—I decided to *believe* him.

He had four more cocktails and told me in detail about how, how often, why, when he talks to the dolphin and does ESP with it. I'm not at all surprised. I do it with you, so why shouldn't he do it with the dolphin? Of course Consciousness is everywhere, a great single immense shining all-encompassing you-know-what, and this funny Yankee is on one of the strands, *in* one of the strands, and his dolphin (called *George,* by the way—such a buddy name!) is in it with him. But then, all things are connected, if only we were clear enough to understand. One day very soon this will be taken for granted, for man will have caught up with himself. Thus spake Adolphe.

One of the marvelous things about dying is that you feel free to follow whatever you are obsessed by. When haven't I been free to do that, I hear you ask, you flea. What I mean is that this freedom becomes *immense.* I'm going to take you with me into that freedom. I'm going to open for you that sea I am swimming in more and more every day, grunting like a walrus, no doubt, and getting lost in the subtle currents—but swimming, and loving the new water, and feeling it *right.* As my body decides to crumble on me, ah my mind, it dances and dances, and in all sorts of novel steps, steps that arrive out of the air . . . You can think me senile if you like (so long as you never dare to say it). Perhaps you would rather I did a rage-and-burn-against-the-dying-of-the-light number, with sermons, denunciations, and train journeys *à la* Tolstoy? Well, I haven't got the wardrobe (or the hair). And the light is *not* dying, it is getting *brighter* in great leaps. I *am* raging, boy am I, but not quite in the sense that that Welshman meant. I wish you could see my poor old cancerous toes at this moment. I've painted each toenail a different color.

I'm not brave. I howl when I'm in pain. But I listen to myself howling from a sort of rickety crystal platform and say, "Brother Ass is howling." And that helps. Anyway, the howling passes. Pain belongs to us also, is part of us, and I am trying to make friends with it. It is amazing what you *can* make friends with if you talk to it on its ground. Enough. And all this from an old hypochondriac whom even a headache once made feel atheistic.

This FREEDOM. I have always, for instance, had a repressed passion for hummingbirds. Now I'm letting it rip . . . It pre-dates my dolphin obsession by two decades. Remember that Brazilian I told you about? The one with the swimmer's pectorals and mouth like Barbara Stanwyck, whom I met in Paris and followed across to Rio for a long hot summer? Well, he had several hundred hummingbirds in his garden, and although I was jealous of them at the time—his eyes would glaze over looking at them, and who on earth could compete with those burning greens and reds and violets, those throats of fire, that delicious *whirr-whirr* of their wings?—I caught some of his passion.

Pondsnipe, as I sprawl here waiting for the Great Raper, as Greta calls him, I've been dreaming of hummingbirds. Perhaps I'll be one in my next life. I don't think they will ever supplant dolphins in my love-life, but they will run them very close, just as in my youth Brazilians were always *numero uno* (that skin! the way their mouths pout from getting round all those Portuguese vowels!), closely followed however by Italians, Yugoslavs, Greeks, Frenchmen, Indonesians, and macaroons.

Guess what! Abdul the Magnificent—who, unlike me, has not taken to his bed despite It All, and totters around Paris talking to pigeons and old ladies and his favorite paintings—Abdul of the Manifold Consciousness and the bad breath (did you notice that Abdul has the worst breath in the western hemisphere?), Abdul my spiritual orgy-brother—we are in constant touch, running, at least shambling, in and out of each other's thoughts, dreams, daydreams, like rabbits—Abdul, without my mentioning *a thing* about my hummingbird passion, found one afternoon on a secondhand bookstall in the rue du Bac something he said on the phone would delight me and make me dream. A book, my dear, on hummingbirds. Of course. *La Vie des colibris,* by the sublimely named pair Ariane Martin and Anne Musy. And on the cover there is a bird who looks just like me on one of my thoughtful days—green gorgeous throat, a purple gown by Elsa Schiaparelli, neck up and long long beak pointed towards the infinite . . . I have been lying here reading about *les colibris,* flying with them, hovering with them, becoming them.

The most fantastical inner transformations seem to be occurring to me as I read. Why has it taken so long for me to recognize myself? I am one of the smallest of the species, *selasphorus,* and I can whirr my wings at no less than two hundred times per second. I have unsuspectedly vast powers of migration. Clouds of me have been seen crossing the Gulf of Mexico in very pesky conditions. Not so far from you, pondy ... So if you see a slightly frazzled but still brilliant bird at the window, you'll know who it is. Say "Selasphorus Adolphus, come in," put out a thimbleful of Californian honey, and see how quickly that sharp Adolphine tongue comes out. Ask it to fly backwards for you and sing "I Get a Kick Out of You" at the same time.

I have much, *much* stranger things to tell you than sitting listening to Americans talk about talking to dolphins and occasionally becoming a hummingbird, and wisdom much larger than the odd remark about befriending pain to share. But I'm tired,—it's three— (nothing serious, old bean, just death), and besides I think I should ladle myself out to you one spoonful at a time. You'll get the whole soup in the end, don't worry— at least, as much as you can take ...

How odd that my life has begun with dying.

What *is* Anna up to, going mum on us like this? I have the highest hopes. Has she run off to Benares with a maharajah? Is she sitting alone on the lower slopes on Nanga Parbat? I'm not sure, but I am sure whatever's going on is at least as interesting as what is happening to us. We are facets of the same crystal. And when one facet turns, the others turn too ... Perhaps we are all going to leave earth together in a chariot, like Ezekiel. I hope it's designed by Erté. Ezekiel's seems terribly uncomfortable. A chariot drawn by hummingbirds; what will I *wear*?

Thank you, by the way, for telling me the dream of yours and Richard's. I knew it. Anna told me before she left that she had dreamt it of you. She was going to tell you, she said, but didn't. Better sometimes we remember for ourselves, although god knows it often takes longer.

Selasphorus

New York

Selasphorus—

I prefer birds of paradise to hummingbirds, but that might be the vulgarity of youth and the fact that the childhood encyclopedia which is the source of anything I know of the animal world had birds of paradise in it in great lurid colors, and not hummingbirds. But I can change and you can change me.

Naturally, I've looked up hummingbirds in various encyclopedias that Antonia has lying about. Where you fly, oh Great One, I plod after, obedient to the end.

Did you know, for instance, that the colors of their feathers are due to physical phenomena of the light's interference—a bit like butterflies' wings? Very good for you, chameleon of chameleons.

And did you know they hibernate? One of the encyclopedias I found is full of stories of finding the little birds dead under bushes high up mountains, putting them in the pocket only to have them miraculously revive. Don't die, hibernate. Ask the hummingbirds in your dreams how to do it.

I met the mother Hughes, and I'm still reeling. I needed four vodkas on re-entry.

Before meeting her I felt both panicked and fed up. I had the clearest resolutions, but they all crumbled in the morning. Of course I wanted to feel clear, open, but all I could somehow remember was my fury at Richard's shame at "us." I remembered the time when he finally confessed to me—in a taxi going up Eighth Avenue— that he was terrified of my meeting any of his family, for what they would see. My god, Adolphe, I don't talk in a high lisp. And even if I did . . . I suppose too he was scared of what I might think of *him* when I met the family that was so mythical to him—the Family, capital F, with their ancient houses and collections of Impressionists and suicides and social pretensions. He wanted me to share his absorption with them, his enslavement to them. Actually to *meet* them would have threatened that, to see that they had pimples and socks like other people, and teeth that needed capping. He wanted to live his lives in separate compartments, to appear as Wonderboy in all sorts of different theaters.

I felt bitter this morning . . . and ridiculous. Why had I played along? What made me bitter was, essentially, not *his* behavior, shabby though it was, but mine. My passivity, my hopelessness. Thank god for you, Adolphe. You have taught me never to be ashamed.

What an absurd situation, to be going to the Veau d'Or to meet the mother of your ex-lover who was always too ashamed of you and of his love for you to introduce you to her . . . I even thought of not turning up at all, of getting the next plane home.

But after equalizing my sideburns, putting on a red shirt, and rereading three of Richard's letters, I went—twenty minutes late. A silly touch that, but somehow necessary. I was trembling as I came down the restaurant steps.

I looked around. She was not there. She, I realized, was doing to me what I had intended to do to her. She was going to be even later than I had been. I should have known I was up against a professional. I amused myself waiting, wondering what she would wear. Cashmere? Silk? Cashmere and silk? Something sober and classy, or something with just a hint of the *outré*, a mem-

73

ory of her lovers in Rome and the famous old poet who had called her neck "round and warm like an old brass bedpost"? . . . I decided she would wear a white silk shirt, a beige woolen suit, and have gloves. Black gloves. She would draw them off and leave them by the side of the plate like large dead leaves . . .

When at last she arrived she was completely different. Is the whole meaning of this new episode in my life to reveal to me that I understand very little? What I had been least prepared for was what seems in retrospect the most obvious thing to expect. Helen Hughes looks very like Richard. The same large sad eyes, the same auburn hair with its different subtle layers of brown, the same almost diaphanous skin, almost too delicate for sunlight. It was from her, as I saw when she sat down, that Richard had got his thin wrists; from her too that he had inherited his quick shaky smile. She wore no jewelry and brought no book. She had only a simple black woolen dress on, and no makeup. She looked worried and haggard.

How could I have imagined she would not look worried? Or worn down? Her son had been in an asylum for a year, and had now disappeared. She was facing me, as nervous and at a loss as he would have been in a similar situation. How could I have thought she would be worldly and commanding? She looked at the world, I saw, with the same eyes as Richard—full of suspicion, the fear that subtle things have of the strong and blundering.

"The train from Boston was late. It often is."

So she had not kept me waiting deliberately.

"Have you ordered? I'm not eating; perhaps a salad." Her voice was higher-pitched than Richard's, but as quiet. "I'm glad you came. I didn't think you would after that letter I wrote. I'm sorry for that letter," she said, looking away. "It seems a little . . . a little ungenerous now. I hope you understand."

I said nothing.

"I have been very unhappy," she said, with such simple desolation that I was startled. Richard might have said it in that way, with the same shocking sincerity of one who does not often speak of his feelings. I felt, I realized, as unprotected before her as I had always felt before him; what a gift they both had of communicating their exposure, of making others feel as exposed as they were, as skinless. She leaned back in her chair and looked at me squarely for the first time.

"You look younger than I had imagined."

"What did you imagine? A lecherous aging schoolmaster with chalk on his shoes?"

She laughed nervously. "I don't know what I imagined. Not you, certainly. I asked Richard once to show me a photograph of you, but he said he didn't have one."

"I don't have one of him either. It was a superstition of our friendship. Exchanging photographs can seem like the end of things, a stealing of the other's soul."

"The Amazon Indians believe that. And they are afraid of mirrors also."

"We are all afraid of mirrors."

"Which is one of the reasons I like this restaurant." She smiled. "The mirrors are at the end of the room. You are not tempted to look into them all the time. My family is very vain. You must have noticed that about Richard. I think he is the vainest of us all. As a teenager he spent hours before the mirror, gazing at himself. Then he had a period when he hated his beauty and the attention it brought him, hated its unmarkedness. 'Mother,' he used to say, 'how can I *look* so calm when I feel what I feel?' And once he told me he wanted to scar himself, disfigure himself, so that no one would look at him with desire."

"He has a small scar under his chin that gets larger somehow when he's tired."

She smiled. "He did that falling off a swing on Cape Cod."

"I know. And perhaps the vainest thing of all is to want *not* to be desired when you look like Richard."

"Richard wants purity. It is his madness."

The salads arrived. We both smiled at the absurdity of the scene—the perfectly tossed salads, the perfect whiteness of the waiter's napkin, the polish of the bar. And Richard's disappearance between us, the final absurdity that had no place here at all.

We tried to eat a little, but both gave up.

"He is alive," I said. "I know. I met an old girlfriend of his yesterday by chance. He rang her last week." And I told her in detail of my meeting with Susan.

"Thank god," she kept saying. "Thank god. Ever since he left I was afraid . . ." She had no need to go on. "You know about my aunt and her death? You know there has been a tradition of . . . disturbance . . . in my family? Of course you know. Why am I asking?"

"You must tell me," I said, "how he has been. How he was in the asylum. How he was when he returned home. I want to know as much as you can bear to tell me. Perhaps in all the details there will be one that will help us—that I will be able to see from a different perspective."

"You sound very professional."

"Perhaps being a private detective will suit me. It might certainly be better paid than being a writer."

"In my divorce from Richard's father I had quite a considerable experience of private detectives, and they are not pleasant."

The prim way in which she said "not pleasant" reminded me that she had an English mother, Richard's grandmother, famous for her chilly rages and judgments.

"You know about the divorce too, I suppose?" Her tone was rather acid. "Richard probably told you everything."

"I don't suppose he knows everything."

"You must meet my ex-husband. I will give you his number before I leave. I wonder what you will make of him."

"And what he will make of me. Does he know?"

"Only God knows what my husband knows. Sometimes I think he has never listened to anything or anyone in his life. Sometimes I think he is the wisest man I know. He may be both, of course. I don't see him very much now. You asked me about Richard. I shall try . . ." She had begun measuredly. She stopped. Her eyes had filled with tears. "Forgive this."

"Don't be stupid."

"I had not intended to be emotional. My friend Caspar James—the poet—says it's my weapon against the world. 'When in doubt, Helen,' he says, 'you cry, and you always win.' Men understand very little."

Her vanity made me smile.

"Richard must have hurt you a great deal," she said.

"No more than I hurt him."

"So you don't resent him?"

"Have you ever been close to anyone without resenting them? Tell me about the asylum."

"I didn't visit him very often. I couldn't bear to. He was very distant whenever I went. You know how he can sit with you and absent himself and make you suffer his absence. Well, he did that often. And he would say just the right things to make me feel guilty. It is not hard to make me feel guilty. Everyone who has known me has known how to. I would try to think of books to take him. He would always already have read them. I would talk about the family and he would cut me short. 'I've finished with them,' he'd say. He can be very cruel, you know. Of course you know. He never changed his clothes, and that depressed me. Always the same worn blue shirt, dirty jeans, dirty sneakers. I think he did it on purpose. Sometimes I used to think, he will look deliberately drab for me. He looked so sad, Charles— so crumpled. You know that look they all get in asylums—crumpled and white and faded out? I'm afraid I was not always kind. How can one be? The mad want to destroy, don't they? They *want* to drag you into their horror. They need to." She paused, out of breath. "How he hated the doctors in there. He thought them idiots. Would not cooperate. Told lies. Invented all sorts of elaborate stories. They despaired of doing anything for him. There were days, though, when I visited him and he was lucid; days when he was clearer than I ever remember him, when there was no suffering in his face or manner, but only a sort of exaltation. My great-grandfather was a rabbi. Richard on those days would look like the painting we have of him. He would talk to me of nature, of the future of mankind. I did not always understand what he was saying, but it did not seem mad. It was on those calm days that he would talk of you.

78

Sometimes rapturously, sometimes . . . with bitterness." She looked at me. "Do you want me to continue?"

"Of course."

"He would say that you understood a great deal, but that you were absorbed by power—your power, that is, your work, your art. He would say that you were always at war with yourself, always torn. That you always wanted to change people, and could never let them become themselves in their own time and rhythm. Sometimes he would say, 'I wish I could help him.'"

I coughed. "And what was he like when he returned home?"

She smiled at my evasion. "Richard is a kind of killer. Perhaps that is why you loved him!"

I said nothing.

"Caspar James and I lived the same story as you and Richard. I'm telling you everything and I'm not even drunk. The same story, except that it was his wife who broke down. We were shrewder; we made someone else pay." She closed her eyes.

"You are not happy," I said. "You paid too."

She waved her hands to close the subject. "Sometimes I have wished," she said, "I could break down. Then perhaps I could break out of myself. Do you never feel that?"

"I saw Richard's suffering. It's hard to feel sentimental about suffering like that."

There was a flash of animosity between us.

She softened. "I deserved that. When Richard returned from the asylum he was quiet. As if they had removed something from him. He has a room at the top of the house, and he would spend days up there listening to Bach and Vivaldi, and not coming down at all, even for meals. I would bring his meals to him, and he would just take them and say nothing at all. He did not seem interested in any of the things he had loved, apart from music. I bought him new books I thought he would like. He would put them at the bottom of the stairs an hour later. I would suggest outings to the theater, the opera. He would refuse them all. He was never harsh or accusing. His distance was more frightening than that. Nothing reached him. Then, after two months, he left. In the middle of the night. There was no letter, no call. I imagined the worst . . . One thing he did do up in his room—he wrote. Notebook after notebook. But in a very odd handwriting that I cannot read. I tried to read it, but gave up. I have the notebooks with me." She leaned down under the table and brought out her large black bag. She placed in front of me three small notebooks, dark beige with coffee stains on them. I opened one.

"Charles, what is it?"

My face must have gone white. For several moments I could not speak. Then I said, "This is my handwriting. This is almost exactly, uncannily, *my* handwriting." I took a piece of paper out of my jacket pocket and wrote a few words out for her, in a shaky hand.

"He has got your *p*'s and *j*'s wrong, but apart from that . . ." She stopped. "Can you read it?"

For a moment I was too chilled to answer. "Yes . . . but not here and not now. You can understand that."

She nodded.

"I think I must go now," I said unsteadily.

Just as unsteadily and with great deliberation she wrote out her ex-husband's number. "Ring him," she said. "What have I brought you into?"

"Not you," I said. "Richard. It's Richard that has brought me here." I don't know why I said that. "Obviously it is him." I felt angry suddenly. "What the hell is he doing?" I must have raised my voice, for the couple at the table behind us looked up and stared. The waiter hovered at an anxious distance. I felt faint. "I'm going now." I left the restaurant.

And then, Adolphe, a frightening thing happened. I was crossing the road, in a daze, and a vast red car seemed to come from nowhere. It winged me and I fell on the pavement. I was not bleeding, just shaken. The car did not stop, naturally. This is New York, after all . . .

So now you have the whole story, up to now.

Except for the notebooks.

Selasphorus, are you ready for this? Find Maria. Put on *Una Voce Poco Fa*. Something very sane, very sparkling.

To have met Helen, seen the handwriting, and nearly been run over in one day . . . thank god there is the "rickety crystal platform" you spoke of in your last letter in all of us, and we can stand there and look down.

You would find all this normal. I keep forgetting that. For you only the extraordinary is ordinary. "It's all a question of categories, pondsnipe." Yes, indeed. But I have a bruise the size of two tarantulas on my hip from that bloody car . . .

There are three notebooks, as I said, six inches by six. Beige, coffee-stained. The paper inside is not lined.

On the question of the handwriting: minuter investigation has revealed certain inconsistencies which make me think it is not my handwriting that he is imitating, but that he is merging his and mine *to create a new hand* altogether. He has kept the basic scribble of my script and many of its consonants. The vowels however are broader. His *o*'s, for example, are much more like *his* *o*'s—very open. His *a*'s too.

81

What does this mean? I remember a graphologist once telling me that consonants expressed the outer, public self, vowels the inner, private one. Perhaps this helps, but I can't yet see *how*.

The first conclusion, then—that Richard was not doing anything simple (however strange) by writing these notebooks this way. He was trying to create something new, to express something absolutely fresh to him. My fear that he was writing *as me* to mimic or destroy me is, I think, my paranoia and not the truth. Something odder is afoot. Does Richard wish in this symbolic way to merge me and him, our two selves and wisdoms, and so create a third person wiser than either of us? And did he write these books *as this third person*? Is this why he seemed so distant to his mother in that period? Because to himself he was *not* himself, but something emergent, something other, a person both him and me and someone else who was the result of him-and-me. I'm sounding like a medieval theologian. I must have some black coffee.

If you think this description of the handwriting is strange, you should read the contents.

They are not "personal." They are not confessions or denunciations or poetic meditations or psychological sketches. They are not letters—to me or anyone else. I have a distinct feeling that he intended them *for* me in some sense, but not—and I do not yet know how to express this—not in a "personal" sense. He is not in these notebooks trying to explain or redress anything.

Some excerpts:

The pit and then the steps out of it. The terror and grace of madness.

It is not simply that the mad accuse society of its heart-lessness, expose people to what they do not wish to acknowledge about themselves. It is that, in certain rare cases, the so-called mad learn things that would, if listened to, compel TOTAL TRANSFORMATION.

Hölderlin visits me and talks to me of the Mothers. [The writing that follows this is excited and illegible, but then, as if by a sudden calming, there appears a clear passage.] It is the era of the Mothers. The Father has gone mad and is trying to eat his children. The Mother is here and fighting to save her children. The Father was only ever half necessary, the fieldworker if you like, the laborer in the field of Being. The Mother is the secret ruler.

Then there follows a series of obscene puns.
There is more, much more on what he calls the Mothers, much of it—to me at any rate—incomprehensible.

I look out of the window and I see Her in the trees on fire.

She is young and is on earth. She is on earth because it is here that Her new revelation is being prepared. Oh the Father will foam and be furious! His foaming is like a waterfall in my ears and I shall have to rest for a while now so it can subside.

Such outpourings, Adolphe, of banality and poetry, what seems like inspired utterance of some kind, and yet . . .
At the end of the second notebook there is a dream—the only dream in the books (which is surprising, because Richard *lives,* or used to, in his dream world). It clearly has to do with this Mother, whatever she is or stands for. It is written very neatly:

At the beginning of the dream Richard was walking through what he immediately recognized as antechambers of the Vatican. He had been to the Vatican with his father as a child, but had not seen these rooms. They were of great beauty, and had on the walls unknown paintings by Raphael and Michelangelo—religious frescoes on subjects he did not recognize, but full of the faces of women. Each of the paintings, however, was in a state of disrepair. It was when he noticed this that he also noticed he was being accompanied by a smallish man in a red robe, with glasses. He looked like a Chinese, but had larger features. He seemed to understand Richard's grief at the state of the frescoes. He also however seemed anxious to help Richard on through the now oppressively decaying and smelly rooms. They came together into a vast courtyard, at least three times as big as the square of St. Peter's.

(At this point, Adolphe, I stopped typing. I was tired and so wanted to refresh myself with some music before I went on. I went to the shelves where Antonia keeps her Callas recordings. I saw a tape, "Callas—Verdi," and put it on, not looking at what I was going to play. Do you know what it turned out to be? The "Ave Maria" from *Otello*. For a moment I felt dizzy. You'll know why when you read on.)

The square was full of a white mist. It cleared slowly as Richard looked into it. He saw in the middle of it a small octagonal brick structure. He was almost shocked at its simplicity. It was not a church or a shrine; it was unlike any structure he had ever seen, any human structure, that is. Its only possible analogy could be found in the photographs he had studied of termitaries of the cells of beehives.

Slowly, as he stared at it, it began to glow and pulse, as if it were some kind of heart.

Richard wished to turn back. But the small man had put his arms around him in such a way that HE COULD NOT TURN ROUND.

A door he had not seen or suspected in one of the front facets of the structure opened and a light shone from it.

Richard began to hear music. He had heard this music once before in the first days of his madness, when it had come upon him quietly like rain. In Ward 19, between the hours of three and four in the morning. Which memory had saved him in his days of trouble.

The music grew louder. A figure was emerging from the door, from the light.

Suddenly Richard was only a few feet from the door and was looking into the face of the figure. It was a woman, a young woman. Wearing a long robe the color of earth.

No. That is wrong. Wearing the earth like a robe. As he looked at the robe, he saw rivers in it, and mountains, and the sun.

He said, "Hail Mary, full of grace," but she smiled. For it was not Mary, or not only Mary, but someone even greater.

Adolphe—I swear to you, as I am your friend and the fool you know, the music I put on five minutes ago was the "Ave Maria" from *Otello*. I didn't even know Maria had recorded it. She never sang Desdemona on stage, did she?

What is happening? I understand nothing. I remember suddenly flashes of that mad evening with Abdul . . . The Kwannon, you stroking the stone woman in the square Georges Cain . . . Do you know something that you are keeping back from me? Forgive me if I sound distraught and not myself, but as you can see . . .

I look around to see if anything in the apartment has altered. The fruit in the black bowl, the curtains, are the same, the table with its glass cover and its hideous Murano glass paperweights . . . they are all the same. I am not having hallucinations. Now you have it all. What on earth (*this* earth) do you make of it?

What is up with Anna?

Charles

I kept the letter for two days because I was afraid to send it. The letter that came from Adolphe two days later through the courier service we were using was therefore one that he had written without knowing what had been happening to me.

ADOLPHE TO CHARLES

Hummingbird—

Not a *word.* What are you keeping under your wings? Abdul has been here with a book on white ants—*The Soul of the White Ant*—but I said to him no. Hummingbirds and dolphins are *quite* enough. I can't change shape every other day. It's too exhausting.

Abdul was miffed. He wants me to become what *he* wants me to become. But he has other virtues of soul and mind which enable me to forgive him that. He tried to seduce me further by telling me of the characteristic and mysterious powers of the queen termite, but his description of her lying prone in a cell giving birth endlessly sounded too much like my present condition to be interesting. One wants to be *different,* doesn't one? I mean, utterly different and other.

Which reminds me. Of what I did not tell you last time. Oh pixie, don't be angry with me for keeping you waiting. How difficult it is sometimes to say the *really* important things. One is frightened of being absurd, or laughed at, or sounding kafutzo to oneself (perhaps that most of all—it doesn't matter that the others think you're nuts, it's when *you* do that the trouble starts).

I often—don't you remember—in our last weeks in Paris dropped hints of something remarkable that was happening to me. I wasn't playing hard to get (I haven't played hard to get since I was twenty-two), I just wanted to tell you when I thought I was ready to tell you, and you were ready, and the forces around us were propitious, and all the inner and outer stars in the right places. What is the point of saying things before their right time? Timing is all . . .

It all began about eight weeks ago. Abdul was sitting in meditation in the Georges Cain on the second bench to the right. It is there, he says, that the forces are strongest. Who can say? When I say "sitting" in meditation, he is of course too plump to sit in the lotus. He just lolls and looks celestial, rather like me but without, I like to think, my flair. His wardrobe, darling! You've seen it. *No* imagination!

It was about four in the afternoon. He went into trance. A very agreeable light crisp little trance, he said, in which the last October roses around the central Flora began to hum slightly. I asked him recently what they were humming, but he doesn't always have his sense of humor, and gave me one of his sting-ray stares.

That afternoon at about five, Abdul rang me: "Something wonderful has just happened."

"You've lost weight? You've decided to change the carpet in that hideous flat of yours?"

"No, you idiot, something *wonderful*."

I resigned myself. He told me about the trance, and then: "When I woke up there was this little man sitting next to me."

"Even at our age all is still possible. Did you tell him you were dying of cancer and really shouldn't strain yourself?"

Abdul, dear Charles, is an old-fashioned prude. I could almost hear his lips pursing. Then he started to laugh. Now when Abdul starts to laugh, as they say in Rider Haggard, Something Is Afoot. He has one of those stagey pantomime laughs, HA HA HA HA, with the accent on the fourth HA.

"I'm bringing him round. Stay there."

"Telling me to stay here, in my current state—" But before I had finished he had hung up.

Well, pondy, go and pour yourself a good strong drink. You'll need it. Guess who this "little man" was? Remember when you were reading *A Burning House* to me I told you about the Tibetan priest that I saw at the Deux Magots, and how he took me to the Musée Guimet and put me before the dancing Shiva there and hit me on the back and sent me off into ecstasy (and all this on a gray Parisian afternoon)? Well, the man on the bench next to Abdul was him, after all these years.

When he came through my white doors with Abdul—who was naturally enough grinning triumphantly—I nearly fainted. It was him, unmistakably—grayer around the temples, thinner, in a crumpled black suit this time, not a robe, but with a Tibetan red shirt; but how shall I describe what happened next without sounding really crackers? I started to cry, pondsnipe, great unforced tears, better than Ingrid in *The Inn of the Sixth Happiness,* better even than Maria Casarès in *Les Enfants du Paradis,* and it is hard to beat that. I wept and wept. Because I was looking into his eyes, looking deep into them, and seeing such love there, such quiet unconditional love, and for me, this lump of feces and facetious imitations that passes for Adolphe in the world (although some, thank god, know better). At last, after all these years, I found out the color of his eyes. Remember I said I could never remember? Well, they are blue. Don't ask me how or why-for. They are blue, that wide white blue of the sky over the Himalayas.

Abdul was dancing from one foot to the other.

"Stop it, you ridiculous elephant," I said, drying my eyes. It was only then I realized the Tibetan had said nothing.

What do you offer the man who has transformed your life? Champagne? Cassis vitelle? I decided on tea.

"Tea would be delightful," the Tibetan said, before I had spoken. He spoke flawless, only slightly accented English, a little slow and ceremonious but perfect.

Before I could stop myself, I found myself asking him where he had learned to speak so well.

He laughed. "Isn't it more important, my dear friend, to ask why I am here?"

He said "my dear friend" like one of those sweet old

colonels with beautiful manners and silken moustaches you used to meet in London clubs.

"I know why you are here," I said suddenly. "You are here to help me die."

"In a way." He smiled, looking at his hands. "But not really."

Abdul coughed and said, "It is time I went now," and before I could stop him had slid out of the room. How fast fat men can be, how noiseless! We were left alone, the Tibetan and I. He came and sat by me on the sofa and held my hand. We had both forgotten about the tea.

We sat saying nothing. I felt this heat, pixie, a throbbing heat spread from his hand throughout my body. It was unlike any warmth I had ever experienced. It penetrated me; I felt it shimmering lightly at the edges of my toes and around the dome of my brain and on the small blue veins of my wrist. I also—this is hard to put exactly—I also felt very large, suddenly, as if my body had dilated to an enormous extent, becoming much bigger than the room we were sitting in. In fact, for one moment, everything—the walls, the Buddhas, the walls of the church opposite—all seemed to be in my body and in this envelope of heat.

I lost any desire to speak (don't smile); I remember noticing I was only just breathing.

It was he who spoke first, and at length. I have asked him if I can tell you what he said, and he says, "It is especially important that he should know." He added, "There is a woman that you both know; it is important she knows also. She, in fact, will understand most clearly of all."

I feel very tired suddenly. What the Tibetan told me is so immense, I feel I cannot express it without betraying it. But if I don't at least *try* to . . ."We are compelled to attempt what is unattainable, to climb where we cannot reach, to speak what we cannot utter." Who wrote that? Did I just write it myself, or do I remember it from theology lessons at school? And why was all this given to me? I've never given up drink except when on antibiotics for the clap; I've never slept naked on rocks except in the South of France, and then handsomely accompanied; I have lived a life of spectacular self-indulgence and frivolity (don't defend me, pondy, it won't be convincing). The only explanation I have been able to come up with for all this is that whoever is Up There has a quixotic sense of fun, and a penchant, *à la* Christ, for low company.

I feel entirely unfitted for and inadequate to what was given me. Is that why it was given to me?

Such questions are of course entirely vain.

What Blue-Eyes said is this: "My dear friend, I am going to tell you something because I believe you to be prepared to hear it. Have faith; open your heart; know that you are perfect in your essence, and be afraid of nothing." Then he sang the mantra of the Buddha of Compassion, "Om Mani Padme Hum," over and over again. I felt a calm descend on my mind and body. It was as if the rocks of his country were singing through him, the rocks, pondy, and the snow on them and the wind blowing between them. I wish I had been wearing something more dignified than my blue Anna-of-Siam bathrobe.

It was funny, while the mantra rang out, to hear the sound of his wristwatch ticking. How lithe and hard his small wrists were, as if they, like his voice, were made of rock! They were hairless like a young boy's.

He turned to fix on me his blue eyes. He looked at that moment exactly as he had looked all those years before, standing outside the Deux Magots. "Adolphe," he began, using my name for the first time, savoring it as if it were a joke between us, "My dear Adolphe, I am now going to take you on a journey. Lie down on the floor."

He took a red cushion from my sofa and put it on the floor about ten inches from his feet. Out of his jacket pocket he took a large dried leaf, which he blessed and put under the cushion.

"You remember," he said softly, "how the Buddha lay when he entered nirvana. Head on his right hand . . . Lie like him."

I am so plump, pixie (let's admit it!), that this is not the most comfortable of positions, but I obeyed. Adolphe in his blue bathrobe lay on the floor of his palazzo in the position of the Buddha entering nirvana.

If I hadn't got *far* more improbable things to tell you, I would just stop here and let you go out and get drunk.

Being me, I asked him where the dried leaf had come from.

"The square Georges Cain," he said.

Blue-Eyes bent down and closed my eyes. I went into what I can only call a waking trance. I was aware of the room around me, of the noises from the street, but my mind became like a screen on which a series of images was projected.

Nothing is more maddening than other people's visions (partly because they make one green with envy), so I won't go on about what I saw. Except for the last part.

I feel like a granny picking out the wing in the chicken

stew and giving it to you with a lot of sauce. Get down on your knees, you wretch, and remember to pray for me every day of your life.

I saw myself entering the square Georges Cain. It was transfigured. The Flora was surrounded by brilliant red roses that glowed with a light from within; the paths seemed made of marble, but of a color I had never seen before, a kind of bluish brown. The leaves that had fallen on them from the trees above all shone separately and distinctly. The whole square was covered in a trellis of rainbows. Thousands of small rainbows intertwined together with the Flora as their center point. Twined transparently so that a great white-blue calmly burning sky could be seen behind them, a sky that had no cloud in it.

You and Anna were there with me, sitting on the grass. You were both dressed all in red, and you were singing together. I wish I could tell you *what* you were singing, but the words were in a language I did not understand—a language with rolling *r*'s and hard *t*'s and sudden open charged vowels.

Anna reached out and held my hand and said, "Whatever you do now, Adolphe, don't talk." As her voice reached me, the light grew around us, so much in fact that we could hardly see each other, for our outlines were almost dissolved in it. I was aware from a rustling sound that there was someone or something else in the square, close to us and getting closer.

Anna gripped my hand. A wave of perfume blew by me. It was so strong I almost fainted. It was a smell I had never encountered before, although it seemed to have mingled in it many of the scents I love most— sandalwood and incense, musk and jasmine and rose, and the lavender that scented my sheets in childhood.

Then the scent passed and the light returned to normal. We were no longer in the square Cain. Or rather, we were, but the place had now dissolved. There was no Flora, no shining roses, no paths of marble, no glowing leaves, no rainbows. There were only the walls around us, stripped of all their ivy and rosettes of stone, stark now and bare. We were seated not on grass but on a soft white sand that filled the whole square.

Our bodies were luminous, pondsnipe, giving off a steady subdued white light, a light like that of a cloudless September afternoon in Paris.

Then the walls were rolled down as if they were only scrolls.

The white sand we were seated on stretched far into the distance.

We sat like this for a long time.

Then on the horizon a small light appeared. It was in the shape of an elliptical egg, like those of some species of hummingbird. For a moment I thought it *was* a hummingbird. It was a reddish orange, and moved with extraordinary shimmering hovering movements, a little above the earth. It was coming towards us.

Wherever it passed, the sand changed color, became charged with the light, took on its reddish-orange luster, and *did not change*. It was as if a scroll of vibrant orange silk were being rolled towards us.

The egg came closer and grew larger. It came to us and folded us in itself. I cannot describe it any other way. It was as if we were folded in it, wrapped in it, penetrated everywhere by its light, which was very delicately warm. We each of us glowed orange-red, not externally but from within. We were not dissolved in the light, but it worked on us somehow, and while allowing us to retain our forms, it changed our essence into its essence.

Anna laughed, I remember, one of her throaty laughs.

When she laughed, the amazing scent returned, even stronger this time, and the egg began turning around us, like a crystal with us in it.

I felt a sudden slap and woke up. Blue-Eyes was standing over me.

"What time is it?"

"What does that matter?"

"Do not speak for a while," he said. "Rest." Then, after a few minutes, he asked, "Tell me what you saw." I told him. He clapped his hands. "You are further on than even I imagined."

"Further on *where*, for goodness' sake?" I was beginning to feel almost testy. What was all this about?

I have a certain vulgar practical side, as you know, and while I had loved every moment of my impersonation of the Buddha, the flashing lights, the webs, the scent, I did want to know now what the hell it was all in aid of. I was, of course, thrilled to imagine I might be "further on." Compliments are *never* wasted on me.

"There is a new force," the Tibetan said abruptly, "and it has entered the world, entered history. It is different from the force of Christ, or the Buddha, or the light and power of any of the known religions."

He said it with such conviction that I felt as if I had been kicked in the stomach. For a moment, despite everything I had received from him even four minutes before, I thought he was stark raving bonkers, and felt afraid. *Really* afraid, as though, if I listened to him anymore, I would myself go mad or become very violent. I wanted to run, but I found I was rooted to where I was standing. Rooted, as if by an immense force. I wanted to shout, but I found, as in a nightmare, that I could not make a sound.

He came up to me and put his face very close to mine, staring into my eyes. I saw the white sands in his eyes, and the small ball of orange light, exactly as I had seen them in my vision. I *saw* them, as I saw his graying temples, the lines of strain about his eyes, the small bloodshot lines around his pupils.

"Do not be afraid," he said. "There is nothing to fear. You are protected."

How tired his voice sounded, mortally tired.

"Reach for what I am about to tell you, not with your mind, for that is worn out and limited, but with your visionary mind which is eternal. We are in Kali-Yuga, my dear friend, the last of the eons, the time of darkness and destruction. The signs are all around us." He tapped me gently on the cheek and my mind was filled with images of all the horror of our time—of a man having his genitalia whipped with cords, of a girl . . . but I do not have to tell you what I saw. Imagine it for yourself— you will have your own images of fear. The last thing I saw was a sea of corpses, a sea stained red with blood, choked with corpses. The sky was dark with sea gulls that plunged and dipped . . .

The Tibetan went on: "Everything is falling away— old cultures, the rites of tenderness between people, the gravity of friendship. The threat of extinction shadows us all and haunts our every thought, whether we acknowledge it or not, making our deepest enterprise absurd. Life has become infernal for most of the earth—

a round of futile pleasures unlit by awareness or real hope, shadowed by the Bomb. Even if the Bomb does not fall, the bombs of apathy, of desolation, have already fallen, and we live in their craters, fleeing into perverse pleasures from our responsibilities towards others." His voice shook.

Then suddenly he laughed, not the high crystalline laugh I had heard earlier but one far earthier, a laugh that seemed to come up through his entire body. "How you people love speeches of doom! How the people of your culture squirm with delight when they are told it is ending! One can almost see your skins flower with pleasure! There is a luxury in doom. Nothing need be done, nothing need be attempted. Work and create a masterpiece? Why? Tomorrow the Bomb will fall. What a relief. Struggle in solitude for enlightenment? Why? Nothing can be done. What a godsend. Secretly, your world is in love with the hopelessness it has fabricated. This is Kali-Yuga, when man falls in love with his own destruction and dances on his own corpse—"

"Look here," I interrupted testily. "I admire you, but I know all this."

Pondy, I was rather proud of myself for that. Shows I do have self-respect after all. If I had feathers, they would have suddenly ruffled.

"Of course. And, knowing all this, you still know nothing."

"There are no depths of ignorance to which I do not sink. I know that."

"That is why you can learn. I want to tell you a story about my master in Tibet. He has gone beyond now, and was already very old when I met him. One day, early in my apprenticeship, I was in despair. I was not progressing in my meditations; I had begun to grasp the pain of what was happening both in my country and in the world. I went to him one evening and poured out my grief. He listened as he always did, with an amused patience that was itself a kind of cure.

"He was sitting in front of a large low table covered with a red cloth and a few sacred objects—a *vajra*, a bell, a bowl or two. 'What do you see here?' he said, pointing to a tiny spot on the far end of the cloth. 'A small crumb of bread,' I said. 'Yes,' he said. 'Consider that this red cloth is the cosmos, the breadcrumb our world. Think how many millions of worlds there are, how much silence among the stars . . . How vain that makes our human misery and complaining!' He watched me as he was talking. 'I see,' he said. 'That kind of talk does not move you at all. Good. The consolations of detachment can be too easy! You are progressing.'

"By now I was thoroughly bewildered. 'But what of the breadcrumb?' He said, 'That is our world, as I said. On this small crumb is where the Buddha manifested himself and revealed to man the secret of his destiny. That is why it ultimately is precious—because it is the place where the worlds can become conscious, where the cosmos can find eyes and ears for itself.'

"'But this is Kali-Yuga,' I said. He laughed. 'Don't you know that in Kali-Yuga there is more chance of enlightenment than ever before? At this time there are many Buddhas, many holy men on the earth to help man. The Bodhisattvas incarnate most at the time of most urgency. It is when the horror is greatest that the chances for enlightenment are greatest.' He blessed me, and passed away two weeks later. So you see," Blue-Eyes said, clearing his throat, "Kali-Yuga is not an end but an opportunity. We are on that small crumb of bread in the cosmos; it is here that enlightenment is possible, here, and always. But there is something even greater, Adolphe, that you should know."

"Let us have some tea," I interrupted. "I desperately need some tea."

"Have you any incense?"

"Of course. Tibetan incense."

"Well then, make the tea and light the incense."

By now, pondy, I was in a state of rather dotty exhilaration. I wanted to sing and dance and do imitations for him. If I had been a juggler or a fire-eater, I would have done a stunning performance just for the hell of it. As it was, I made some tea and poured it into those black Japanese cups Anna gave me for my last birthday.

You should have seen the way Blue-Eyes drank his tea, by the way—not at all as the priests do it in that Ronald Colman film about the Tibetan valley, as if they were in some heavenly Ritz, but very noisily indeed, smacking his lips.

Look, pondy. I've had a wonderful time writing all this to you, as you can imagine, but I'm not sure I have the strength at this second to tell you what happened next. I'm not playing Perils of Pauline, leaving you clinging by a fingernail to the cliff of gnosis—I'm just exhausted. Besides, haven't you had enough of Blue-Eyes and Adolphe and orange light and Wisdom (capital W, fanfare of sackbuts and shawms) for a bit? I know your appetite for me is endless (it's your chief charm), but even you must be fully fed by now. Of course what I'm *not* telling you yet is by far the maddest bit, the bit that even I still have trouble with. Not trouble exactly. Whenever I talk about it to myself I think I've finally lost it.

99

What have I found by losing it? You will judge. But not now.

Now is four o'clock. Time for those fat green pills and a lunge at sleep. I will tell you one thing, though, that Blue-Eyes said. We talked about you, and us, and he said . . . (Promise me you will read this bit calmly, with your hands on your hips, aware of all the good powers that surround you.) He says you are in danger because you are very close to something momentous in your life.

I did not want to tell you before. I didn't want to alarm or discourage you. You must know by now that everything you and I are experiencing is threaded together. In a sense I am paying for what I am learning, with my life. I told you that, remember, when I said that my cancer dates from almost the time I first met the Tibetan, and he gave me the vision that changed everything for me. There are obviously great karmic obstacles in my past that make it necessary for me to pay this way, and I couldn't care less at this point. The bloody gods of karma can have my fat exhausted old body and good riddance. But you are young(ish); you are frail, spiritually, still inexperienced. The closer we come to Truth, the more the dark powers in us and around us cluster about, to try to prevent us from reaching it. Their malevolence can be used to further our search; their fury can be turned into a source of power for love and clarity; but that takes, god knows, awareness, and shrewdness, and a diamantine savvy. Keep your savvy diamantine. WATCH OUT.

I dreamt last night you had had an accident of some kind. Can this be true?

Through everything be cheerful and heroic
like your old
wondergran

100

New York

Your amazing last letter crossed mine about Helen Hughes and the notebooks, etc. Now you will know what an odd dimension everything has moved into here. What can I say about your letter? I'm reeling. I'm expectant. I don't wholly understand, but understanding seems beside the point.

I am patient for "what happens next." I know you think I'm the most impatient creature on earth, but that is not wholly true (and perhaps a projection, dare I say it?).

When are we going to find out what Anna is up to? Here we are, being worked on by whatever-it-is, spilling the beans to each other, and we don't even have an address to get to her at. I, like you, feel her silence is hatching something. And having just written that, I also feel that when we find out we will be very sustained in what we are undertaking.

What exactly *are* we undertaking? I wouldn't like to try and be precise about *that*. Imagine having to get up in front of a roomful of dons and defend a syllable or moment of what we have been saying or doing! I'd rather commit hara-kiri with a blunt kitchen knife.

Adolphe, about danger—you will know now about the red car that nearly ran me over when I stumbled out of the Veau d'Or. I have dreamt about it both these last nights. And in both dreams I have seen the driver. It is a young woman, foreign-looking, dark and wearing dark glasses. I also have the very odd impression that although, whoever she is, she wants to run me over, she means no harm by it. That in fact if I *was* run over, *really* run over, flattened and squashed and pulped, some-

101

thing astonishing would happen. In both dreams the car does hit me and I explode.

Of course, this may just be compensation for the fear I felt when reading what Blue-Eyes had said. Actually, I already knew it. The time is dangerous.

At the same time as being afraid, I also feel reckless and lighthearted. Dare I write "I will pay whatever price gladly"? If I do, what Fates are listening?

The red tongue of Antonia's Kali is redder than ever this evening. I have taken to watering it every day. A little drop of olive oil . . .

Don't worry, I'm not losing my marbles. I'm *collecting* them. What have I been doing these last days? I have locked myself away up here with Richard's notebooks and my memories of Richard.

I have this feeling that I cannot find Richard, or begin to know where to look, until I have found him in myself and looked at him clearly. That two activities, internal and external, are not only connected. They are the same. He is where I will find him in myself. We were that close. Close—what an inadequate, *bourgeois* little word. We *were* each other at moments.

How can I have forgotten those moments? Another ridiculous question. It is hard to remember the beautiful, the extraordinary. Even now as I am re-experiencing those moments with delight, there is a part of me wishing that they would end and fade. How strong that part is. It is ignorance itself, the sophisticated core of ignorance that invents every reason for disbelief, irony, and safety.

Two memories return again and again. In the first, Richard and I were in my rooms in Rhodes, the town in upstate New York where we met. It was snowing outside and we were listening to the *Missa Solemnis*. Richard had never heard it before. He grew more and more agitated, opening books and then putting them down, walking to the window. "This is terrible," he kept repeating. At one point quite early in the work he looked so scared that I said, "Shall I turn it off?" "No," he said. "I must listen to the end," with the kind of passion appropriate to an ordeal, a rite of passage. We came in the music to that passage where Beethoven changes key completely for the "Et incarnatus est," "And was made incarnate," "ex spiritu sancto, ex Maria Virgine," "by the Holy Spirit, out of the Virgin Mary"—that passage which is like a vast quiet wind from another world . . . Richard stood up as if in a trance. No, he *was* in a trance. His face was completely changed, Adolphe. Once before I had seen him in the hour before he had an attack, desperately trying to fight it, his eyes full of fear; I had held him, and the attack had passed him by. This time was different; his face was full of joy. But I was as afraid for him in this state as I had been in the other. It was so extreme, so undefended, as open and naked as the music, as defenseless. I can see Anna raising her eyebrows and you gazing up at the ceiling ("Really, this is too much—visions to the *Missa Solemnis*—*so* nineteenth century"), but I am only reporting what I experienced. I went and stood behind him and put my hand on his heart—my right hand.

With his right hand Richard covered mine and pressed it hard.

I entered for a few moments Richard's state of soul. Yes, that is what happened. I was not feeling with my mind and heart, but with his, and completely, Adolphe, without any barrier.

I felt it was his power that created this union.

I had forgotten all this until now. How much I have buried.

The second memory: a conversation Richard and I had the day after one of his attacks. It was a Sunday; I was working in the long cold office the university had given me. I heard Richard calling me from under my window. He looked very pale and thin in his large black coat against the background of the snow, but he had his flute with him. When I came to the window, he played for me. I opened the window and the notes fell on my face with the freshness of the air off the snow.

He came in and we talked. It was then that he told me of the orange light he saw sometimes in his attacks. "They are not just cruel, these attacks, although even the 'good' ones leave me exhausted. Often I feel as if I am being *used*, as if there is some power that is trying to contact me, to dance in me and flow through me." He looked at my face to see if there was any trace of fear or scorn in it.

"Go on," I said. "I have never experienced anything like what you are saying, but I believe it is possible."

He smiled at my precise caution. "I know," he said. "That is why you are the only one I trust."

I was sitting in my chair at the desk. He sat on the desk and crossed his legs. He picked up his flute and played me something I did not recognize.

We were alone in the large house. No one else was working there that Sunday. Outside the afternoon light was white and shining. It seemed to stream back off the snow, refreshed, and fill the room. When he had finished he put his hands around my neck.

"What were you playing?"

"Charles always wants a name, a place, a date, an explanation."

"I can't help it. I'm English."

He mimicked me. "I can't help it. I'm English! I'm an American. I can live in mystery and not be afraid." Richard was given to grand quotations; I remembered the time he read *Walden* to me in a cemetery.

"You're as much of a fraud as I am," I said. "What were you playing?"

"I was playing the music I always hear before it happens."

"Before what happens?"

"Before whatever it is tries to get hold of me and use me. Sometimes I give in, sometimes I don't. That music is what I always hear. I've listened to Persian and Indian things," he said, "to Chinese and Japanese flute music, but it is none of those."

I asked him what happened in his attacks.

"I've told you about the bad ones. The good ones are more various ... Sometimes they are stories, like dreams. I am taken to a wood by figures in white, or to a broken-down temple, or to the edge of the sea. I am told to do something to purify myself. Sometimes it is painful. Once I had to hold my hand in a flame until all the lines in my palm were charred. Another time I had to roll on a bed of sharp white stones until I bled all over. When this process is over, it starts. It starts with a kind of humming that seems to be coming from everything. As if a thousand thousand tops were spinning." He looked at me anxiously. I nodded to him to go on.

"When I am in harmony with this sound all around me, the light begins. Sometimes I see it coming towards me from the horizon. A small star, say, that grows larger and larger and pervades everything, soaks everything with its light. Sometimes it just seeps up from things themselves, as if they had kept it hidden, and now, because I am singing, the sound reveals it to me. Things are so marvelous, Charles, in that light. A stone, for instance, starts to dance. *Dance* is a bad word. You see it shaking in all directions, exploding, and yet staying in the same place at the same time. All matter is charged with this light. When I am humming, I am charged with it too. It begins at the bottom of the body and I can see it rising—up my legs, through my genitals, up to my head . . . It comes from outside and meets itself coming up from inside. It is both exterior and interior. When it reaches my heart I begin to be frightened. It is so hot suddenly. It's a difficult heat to describe. I don't feel as if I am going to be burned, exactly; I feel as if I am going to faint *into* it, to become it. And that if I do, I will cease to exist, or be conscious, at all. But the light rises. And then . . ."

"The terror starts," I said.

His face was very pale. "Yes. It is physically as well as mentally painful. It is painful because I am not ready for it. I am too young, too egocentric, to receive it completely. Do you understand? I fight it and then it almost kills me. But just before the terror begins, I fall into this heat and writhe in it—that is the only way of saying it; I writhe in it like a snake you have hit on the back with a stick—I feel a peace, as great as the heat and threaded into it." He paused. "You should ask me now, 'What is the light?' That would be like you."

"What is the light?" I smiled.

"Give me an idea of the kind of answer you would respect." His voice was sardonic suddenly.

"Richard, trust me. You have taken me into a territory I have no experience of. I believe you are telling me the truth. I love you."

"You and your love, your *love*," he began, but seeing the fear in my face he stopped. "Don't let us get into that."

"No."

"I do not know what the light is. And I do not know what the power that sends it is. I think it is a new light, something new." He shook his head at himself and smiled. "How odd that sounds. A new light, something new."

"Does the experience itself give you no clues?"

He laughed. "I think the light is feminine."

"Well, my dear chap, that does sound a little far-fetched."

"A little? I do not know why I think it is feminine. I feel it. I forgot to tell you that the figures that lead me to the place of purification, or whatever it is, are always women. *Always*. Usually old women, ancient even, sometimes, but always beautiful. As I imagine the sibyls to have been."

"Not all of them. There was one who was kept in a cage and refused death, who looked like a grasshopper."

"You *would* remember that. The light is orange; it is a new light, a new force, and it is feminine. Is that precise enough for you?" He got up off the desk. "Sometimes I think my madness is a battleground, between the earth and this light, between all the things that do not want to change and this light that wants to change everything. That my psyche is one of the million places that this fight is being fought out. Will you ever speak to me again after that?"

I was very moved by what he was saying. But I was as baffled as I was moved, baffled and scared. So I changed the subject. We never spoke of the light again.

In fact, I wonder if I would have remembered it had you not written me your letter and your experience with Blue-Eyes.

Something is starting to become clear about Richard, his madness, the notebooks, his disappearance . . . I open one of Richard's notebooks at random. I do that often these days. When I want to "hear" Richard, I open his book.

> Man is at a preliminary stage. He is a sketch for the painting he is to become, a squiggle still on the canvas of eternity.

Underneath Richard has done a self-portrait, "Richard as squiggle. In it one eye is dark, as if it were full of blood. You cannot see its pupil. The other is much vaster, and open, staring full ahead. It is like the eye of a Byzantine Christ, the Christ, say, of Dafne, the Resurrected Christ. And around the rim of the eye—it is a drawing—around the rim Richard has put in a wavy orange line that in places is throwing out tentacles towards the center. A kind of orange web, but growing from the outside in . . . Under it he has written, "God knows what will happen when the *pupil* is orange."

I left a gap there because something happened then. I was about to sign off when the phone rang. Usually I don't answer Antonia's phone, except when she rings me, which is regularly every evening at seven (you know how organized Antonia is . . . in *some* things). This time I went over and picked it up.

"Antonia. How are you, old witch?" A gravelly male drawl.

"Antonia isn't here. This is a friend of hers. Can I give her a message?"

"Where the hell is she? I wanted to take her to the PEN celebration tomorrow."

I recognized the voice. It was Carl Huston, lanky Carl of the legendary local reputation, based on two anorexic collections of short stories.

I had forgotten Antonia knew him. I knew him too. He had been a visiting writer at the campus where I met Richard. He was the campus demon, the hired flail of the Children of Mammon. His classes were legendary for their length and emotional violence. Richard had been his favorite pupil.

"Carl," I said uneasily. "Hello. How good to hear you. This is Charles Hallam."

"Richard Hughes's friend."

"Yes."

"Richard's friend and mentor." He said the word *mentor* ironically.

"If you like." I asked him if I could come and see him about Richard "as soon as was convenient." Something very serious had happened which I could only explain in person. I am not usually so determined, but I wanted suddenly to see Carl, badly. I flattered him; I said I had read his latest story in *The New Yorker* (which I had) and that I had admired it (which was only partly true).

"You have taste, Charles Hallam. We can always rely on the Brits to have taste."

The way Carl said the word *taste* was not calculated to charm.

Then his voice relaxed. "I remember Sophie liked

109

you." (Sophie is his wife.) "Yeah, Sophie thought you were cute. Why don't you come over tonight? We're having the usual crowd. A select sprinkling of the *crème de la crème*. You wouldn't be too out of place. Come an hour early, at seven. We'll go up into my eyrie and talk."

"I need to talk about Richard."

There was a pause.

"I guess we both need to talk about Richard. What a gift the boy had."

"What kind of gift do you mean?"

"The most interesting one. The gift for destruction."

Of course I went. Surprisingly, the memory of Carl that came back to me as I walked across Central Park to his flat in the Majestic was a gentle one. He, Richard, and I had gone out one summer evening to one of the waterfalls outside the town where we were living and skinny-dipped together and sat until it was dark on the rocks in the shallows, talking. Carl had been benign that evening; the harsh lines in his face had relaxed, and his habitual irony was touched with a warmth I had not seen before. He had talked of his boyhood on a poor farm in the Midwest, and Richard had said afterwards, "Did you notice how beautiful Carl was when he was speaking?"

"Yes," I said, "but New York will make him cruel again."

It was a shrewd card to play. Richard feared New York; for him it was Babylon, the abomination of abominations.

Remembering the evening and our comments on it, I was shocked at myself, at how much I had wanted Richard for myself. Had Carl too wanted Richard for himself? Two ersatz Socrateses fighting for a nervy oddball Phaedrus . . . The scenario had its amusing edge. Carl had been mostly wary with me, but I had felt a certain friendship from him. He had given me his first book of stories with a dedication, "To the man who likes Proust too much but has the balls to love Faulkner." Balls came into almost every conversation with Carl. Nabokov had balls; Updike didn't, and never could have had; Saul Bellow *might* have had balls, if he hadn't . . . etc., etc. One of Antonia's epigrams: "Carl *does* have balls. Made of papier-mâché soaked in strychnine."

Carl met me at the door of his apartment, dressed completely in black, with a silver chain round his neck. He looked much older than I remembered him, more grizzled around the temples, shorter somehow, almost wizened. I had never noticed before the slight twitch in the right side of his face. His eyes flickered with their familiar tension and irony.

"Well, English, you've finally entered the twentieth century."

"What do you mean?"

"Your clothes, English. Paree is good for you. I'm glad you've given up the silk scarves. They were a little too Wilde for comfort."

"Carl, it is always a pleasure to see you. So direct, so quickly."

He smiled. Carl is like a wrestler. He likes the other to fight back. I suddenly wished I'd had a couple of vodkas to oil my brain.

I glanced round at the apartment. It was black and white: black table, black carpet, white walls. *White* walls. Everything neat, shiny. Nothing on the walls but one Jasper Johns circle, in green, with frayed, tense edges.

"Come to the window, English. I want to show you John Lennon's white piano."

The flat looks over into the Dakota, into the flat where John Lennon lived with Yoko Ono.

"Never saw him play it, English. I kinda like this flat, having so much black, and that being almost all white. Two keys on the cosmic piano of New York. Good phrase, English, don't you think? You can have it."

"Thank you, Carl. I need all the good phrases I can get."

"Sometimes I think I should leave New York. But where would I go? London? Theroux lives in London, which is one reason for never visiting, let alone living there. Imagine having those sentences washing over you in your sleep. Reading Theroux is like being trampled to death by geese."

I noticed the large empty tumbler in Carl's hand. He had given himself an unfair advantage.

"Carl, before you run through all the world's capital cities and the whole New York intelligentsia—"

"There is no New York intelligentsia. You'll see. They'll all be here in an hour."

"Carl, give me a drink. Is that direct enough? A large drink."

"My, my, English, have you learned to drink too in Paree? You used to start swaying after one martini. Swaying and talking about Proust. I hope Paree has cured you of Proust, anyway." He pronounced it *Proooost*. He went to the black lacquer cabinet, got out the vodka, and poured me a stiff one. "Actually, English, I like Proust. I wish he'd known me. I'd have said, 'Marcel, more vice, baby, more *steam*, less diddling over church spires. Less celestial phallus worship and more *action*. I'm just a vulgar American from the boondocks, but I like action.'"

"Liar. Nothing happens in your stories, and that is why they are good."

"A little slick, English, but not bad. Here's to you."

We sat in silence. I felt Carl was exhausted for some reason, but before sympathy and vodka made me too unwary, I remembered that Carl worn could be even more cruel than Carl exuberant. Slumped in the black Swedish steel chair, he looked like Tiberius after a day's unsatisfying debauch.

There are very few times, Adolphe, when I am nostalgic for England and its shabby nobilities. Sitting there with Carl in his chic cage was one of them.

"We haven't even mentioned Richard's name," I said.

"Very English of us, don't you think? Richard. Beautiful Richard of the eyes. Did he train those eyes on you too? That stare, that Garbo stare, that "I am lost, rescue me if you dare" stare. Richard. That is three times I have said his name in as many sentences. What more do you want?"

I said nothing. I did not know what I wanted.

Carl went and poured himself another large vodka, burped melodramatically, and sat down.

"Actually," he said, "I hate Jasper Johns. I put it up there to annoy people. It's worth a million dollars."

"Good for it."

"You're above lucre, aren't you?"

"Beneath, a long way beneath. Back to Richard."

"What a good title that would be. Back to Richard. Back to Richard's backside. Sorry about that. Vulgar."

"And inaccurate."

"To be both vulgar and inaccurate in one sentence takes . . . takes Norman Mailer. Sorry about that too. Norman and I are now friends, you know."

"Really. Do you arm-wrestle?"

"Even in America, straight men of a certain age can talk to each other."

"How straight are you, Carl?"

"You've heard the stories. They are true, English, true. I went with the boys, as they say, in the early days. I was cute as hell and I enjoyed it. But I always liked women more. More subservient. Always willing to immolate themselves on my pyre. Try getting a boy to immolate himself. He's too busy looking in the mirror and trying to get into modeling."

I had had enough. "I think I'll go now," I said, standing up. "I can meet the nonexistent intelligentsia another day."

"You're not going," drawled Carl. "You're going to stay and listen to your old friend Carl. I have some very juicy bits for you, baby, very juicy. Don't you want to know what Carl knows?"

He seemed fearful, leaning back there, drunk, talking in his eerie baby-voice, rubbing his glass up and down his thigh. What would Anna do?

She would cross her legs and fix her eyes on him.

I crossed my legs and fixed my eyes on him. "I'm sure whatever information you have to give me about Richard will be very enlightening."

Good old Anna.

"And very stimulating."

Stimulating was a touch of genius only Anna could have managed.

"It will be stimulating all right, English. Grip your drink and here goes ... Shall I put what I have to say baldly, in the modern idiom, or shall I ramble around it *à la* James?

"Ramble."

"I'll ramble a bit and then get bald. Technically better, more deadly."

"You want to be deadly?"

"I think so. One must have one's pleasures. Why write when you can kill? That is why I love teaching so much. All those sweet soft little minds, lying like lamb's brains on a plate, waiting to be sliced."

Carl started to pace the apartment. "To Richard, then. To Richard and you. What an odd, fetching pair you made! *Fetching* is such a good word. Everyone thought so. Not that you were a pair, of course. But you were seen everywhere, gazing into each other's eyes, walking in tandem, eating at the smelly old Greek restaurant downtown, your two overlarge black coats nuzzling each other in the winter wind. That relationship of yours, English, was quite the talk of campus. I'm sure you're honored. I mean, to be the talk of *that* campus. For one long stiflingly dull winter you were the talk of the town. '*Are* they or *aren't* they?' was the gist of it, and then, 'Where?' and 'How often?' Very sophisticated stuff. *Very* sophisticated places, campuses, as you know. You were cast as the visiting English villain and Richard the helpless American innocent about to be perverted into wicked European ways. The young Boris Karloff and Mr. Ralph Lauren. I fed the fire whenever I could."

"I can imagine."

"I said you listened to Beethoven in your briefs and read Kafka to each other over crêpes Suzette. I said that you had tried wrestling in the nude like in *Women in Love*, but American hash won too easily over British sausage, and you got piqued and went sternly back to Kafka. Not all of my allusions worked. Too many structuralists about who don't read. I had a good time. As good a time as you can have in that place. Someday someone will succeed in being happy in that town, and the whole place will go up in smoke . . . Do you know how many suicides there were there last winter during my 'Death and Decadence' course? No connection, I'm sorry to say. Twelve. *Twelve* young idiots plunged to their deaths in one icy Coca-Cola–littered gorge or another. They call it 'gorging' up there. Witty for the United States of Aerobics, don't you think? Oh, that place where we first met, so memorably—will I ever be done singing its praises?" Carl paused and raised his glass. "To the Place by the Lake! I bless every imitation Oxford stone of you, every masturbator in the library lavatories, I bless every living structuralist. Long may the destruction of meaning continue! May no one ever read anything but critics on critics, so I no longer have to pretend to write! Don't worry, English. I'm not forgetting you and Richard. Just filling in the picture."

"I remember the picture. And the toast."

"I'm sorry to repeat myself."

"Not sorry enough. I want to know what you are keeping back about Richard."

"Slowly, slowly. You were a fetching, much-talked-about pair. Okay. Enough rambling, let's get bald."

"You are going to enjoy this."

"Not as much as you think, perhaps." Carl's voice shrank to a tired whisper. "Don't worry about the guests. There aren't any. I canceled the party. Sophie has gone to the new Woody Allen to get some sleep. I wanted to be alone with you."

"Why?"

"You'll see in a minute. Perhaps I will enjoy this. Unveiling the statue to you will be interesting. I will watch your face. To see if you really are English. To see if you do have a stiff upper lip."

I stood up. "I think I should go."

"That's the second time you've done that. How many exit lines do you need? No, you won't go until you know everything." He added softly: "Richard fucked us both over. He is good at fucking people over. A real professional."

I sat down.

"I believed in Richard," Carl began. "That is for once the right word. I *believed* in him. He was everything I had wanted to be when young—privileged, beautiful, athletic, and flute-playing. The most brilliant pupil I have had in all my years there. Other people in the department thought him slow; I saw that he had a unique mind, very poetic and wayward. So far I'm only telling you things you know."

"Get to the point."

"There are three points," he said slowly, with a smile. "Three points, as there were twelve suicides. Numbers are important. The first is that all the time you were in love with Richard he was sleeping with me, on and off. The second is that he was afraid of and largely disliked you. He said so often, at length, and with considerable subtlety. The third is that he was also, unknown to me, going down to New York from time to time (you must remember the times) to sleep with Sophie, my wife. He had a very active year. He managed to lie to you, make me unfaithful for the first time in ten years, and cuckold me all at the same time. He killed both his fathers and fucked his mother. Would Freudians call that a success?"

"You are lying."

"I was afraid you would say that. I hoped you wouldn't, because I would have retained some respect for you. I am not lying. No one could invent what I have just told you. It is too rococo, even for an old hand like me! Remember that evening we all went to the waterfall? I talked lyrically about my childhood. We all took our clothes off. It was very Huck-on-the-riverish! After we dropped you, we went to your office and fucked in it."

I said nothing.

"Did you or did you not have Richard make a key for your office so he could go and work there?"

"Yes."

"Well then. You had a good long desk. The place was empty and the boy was willing. We were doing no one any harm."

"I will go now," I said slowly, trying to find the words. How hollow the voice sounded.

"Aren't you going to finish your vodka? You should never leave good Russian vodka."

I picked up my glass and emptied it slowly onto the floor. It was a pathetic gesture and I am not proud of it. Then I walked out.

I don't know how long I walked, Adolphe. It is five in the morning now and I must have left Carl's around ten. Everything that Carl said seemed suddenly likely— Richard had admired him, I knew that, talked about him obsessively. Richard had often said how beautiful Sophie was. Richard could easily have found it easier, more re-assuring, to sleep with Carl than with me. He could even have wanted him. Carl was compelling. Richard could have wanted to revenge himself on us both by sleeping with Sophie, who would have had her own motives for hurting Carl.

I felt sick.

If Richard had done that . . . then everything he and I had been was without any of the meanings I have given to it, and everything I have been thinking these last days is nonsense, feverish rubbish . . .

I understand at last a little of what your Tibetan might mean by danger. The scope and range of it. Danger not just from without, but from within. From within, and so most dangerous . . .

When I was on the point of despairing about everything, I heard Anna's voice *as if from beside me* (I was stumbling up Fifth Avenue near the Guggenheim): "I don't believe it. I do *not* believe it. Go over each detail."

I said, "I have, I have," as if to her.

"Don't give Richard up too easily. *Go over each detail.*"

I went over each detail, each thread in Carl's story. Then I got it. The key. Literally. Yes, I had given Richard the key to my office door, and he did use the office to work in sometimes when I wasn't there. But he had *lost* it, Adolphe. He had lost it about two months after I gave it to him, which is about a month before the expedition to the waterfall with Carl. I know, because I found him sitting grinning once outside my door. And then, suddenly, I remembered something else, something about that evening by the waterfall. Richard and I had left Carl at his flat and walked home. Why do I remember it? Because he and I had a quarrel. It was about the most ridiculous thing—it was about (oh god) whether women looked better in men's sweaters than men did. I said they did, often, and he said they never did. We both sulked and stamped, then hugged and got drunk. How could I have forgotten that?

I laughed out loud. After I'd finished laughing, a new

doubt shook me. Perhaps I had remembered it wrong? I heard Anna mocking me: "Will you never trust anything? Never? Never?"

Why had Carl done what he did? Why? Had he made a pass at Richard and been refused? Had he seen what Richard and I felt for each other and wanted to destroy it? I'm tired, Adolphe. I don't want to think about Carl.

Sudden realization: Carl, by lying so brilliantly, has made me aware of all my hidden fears about Richard, of all the suspicions that I have kept from myself. His malice spun them into a shape that would have destroyed me if . . . if they had been true.

But they are not. Richard has hysterias and vanities, but he is basically good. Everything stands on that. By his cruelty Carl has purified me of my madness.

I was going to see Richard's father tomorrow. I will put him off a day. I need a day to be with Richard as I have found him again.

Charles

ADOLPHE TO CHARLES

Banana, pondy, periwinkle—

I feel I must call you all your heavenly names because you have come through a whopper of a test. At first I thought, he's making all this up. He's testing his old gran to see if she's still *compos mentis*. Too mad even for New York. But nothing is too mad for New York, or anywhere else for that matter.

I am really too old to find evil interesting. I suppose

that shows just how old and ill and tired etcetera I am. But on the other hand evil isn't really *that* inventive, you know. Its motives are too narrow.

Three Adolpheisms on goodness to cheer you up:

Goodness wins against evil because it refuses to play.

Goodness triumphs even when defeated because it does not know or want to know the meaning of victory.

Two's quite enough, I think you will agree. I can go on like this for hours.

I feel ridiculously blithe. Don't feel I am being heartless; I know, I *know* how much you must have been through. I *feel* it—look, the gray hair on my arms is tingling. It's just that I know too that you are tough and that you will learn from this, and also that the Carls of this world have already lost.

How sad to have already lost.

Enough of *him*.

If you ever write the scene up, for god's sake break that vodka glass over his head.

As Ramakrishna said to the cobra, "One is not, Brother Cobra, allowed to bite. But one *is* permitted to hiss."

Hiss away. I have a famous hiss, as you know. It's been so loud on occasions it could blot out the finale of Beethoven's Ninth.

I think you are ready to hear now the rest of what the Tibetan told me. Anna has written us a joint letter which I am sending with this. DON'T READ IT TILL THE END. I want the stage all to myself.

By the way, what you said at the end of your letter was almost wise. I read it twice, just to make sure I wasn't writing it myself. Yes, Carl has given you a great gift. He has given you the gift of your own jealousy, your own fantasy. He has made you see what you think Richard capable of. God knows what must have run through your mind sometimes in those months of love. Murder, at the very least. All very normal. The diamond is in the shit, as the tantric masters say. The rose flowers from dung. Lots of dung about.

If you are going to find Richard, as you say, in yourself, you have also to look at that grisly possessive clawing mean-souled insecure vampire of a self. Put on your helmet. Down into the mine, old bean, down into the mine.

Now to our Tibetan. In my last letter (you have it by heart, I hope) I left Wondergran and Blue-Eyes sipping Lapsang Souchong.

Do you know what unworthy thought crossed my mind as I sipped? "Please, Blue-Eyes, give Odile de Valois who lives beneath me and has for years done nothing but tell wicked stories about me, give her an A-grade, mind-splintering vision and vindicate your servant Adolphe." You see, pondy, my ego is definitely *not* dead.

Blue-Eyes finished his tea, clapped his hands, and said, "It is time now to throw away everything you have ever known or imagined you knew."

I have to say I giggled.

"My dear friend," I said (*everything* about Blue-Eyes is catching, even his way of talking), "that won't be nearly as hard as it is supposed to be. I've even forgotten the names of most of my own films."

"That shows a certain taste," the Tibetan said. "I've seen them all, you know. It is the one thing in our association that I have found less than delightful."

"Less even than the tea?"

"About the same."

Blue-Eyes stood up. One of the odd things about Blue-Eyes is that he seems much taller at certain times than at others. This was one of his tall moments. He has this knack, too, of making his eyes pierce. It's a little melodramatic, but then, why not? Even the holy need a few props. Maybe he's learnt it from one of my films.

What a thought, pixie. A thousand years of purgatory, at least. He fixed me with his eyes. I shook inwardly, but held his gaze.

"Up to now," he began, "man has had essentially two limited visions of his evolution—the Western and the Eastern, the Darwinian and the Cyclic."

"Explain," I said. "Remember you are talking to an aging cretin."

He sighed. "My dear friend, do not call yourself such names. Remember you are perfect."

"I may be perfect in one sense," I said stubbornly, "but I am an aging cretin."

"Supposing *both* were wrong?" he went on. "Both the Darwinian belief in the survival of the fittest, of man as a chance creation having to keep struggling for his survival, and the Cyclic—the tradition I was reared in—with its vision of time forever turning upon itself?"

"Look," I interrupted, "I shall have to sit down at this rate."

We sat down together on the sofa.

"The West," he began again, "has celebrated matter. The East has celebrated spirit. Both celebrations have involved losses, omissions, necessary oblivions."

"Slowly," I warned. "Slowly."

"The West has believed in certain of its philosophies— such as Marxism—that history is tending to an apotheosis of man. This is a moving vision except for one thing:

its vision of that apotheosis is material. Man's spiritual needs are ignored. His consciousness, in other words, remains essentially the same, although freed by freedom from social injustice to know a greater fellow-feeling and identification with others."

"My, my," I said. "You *have* been doing your reading."

"This is why I came to the West," he said simply, "to appreciate it, to learn from it."

He said this with such earnestness I was touched. "You mean this tired old whore of a civilization still has something to teach you mountain sages?"

He ignored my facetiousness. "The East has also had its noble vision of man, a vision that still endures. In this vision man is godlike in his being, and able to participate in the being of God and so be released from the pain of the world, the wheel of time. There are many names for this release, this ecstasy, in Eastern philosophy—nirvana, moksha. But this vision has the disadvantage of depreciating the world, of finding it too readily a sink of iniquity."

"One of my favorite phrases."

"This is getting nowhere," he said. "I'm even boring myself. I will tell it to you straight, without justifications, in all its madness. That way, you will have to decide for yourself."

"My mind may be too small."

"Your mind, my dear friend, is as small as you want it to be."

The Tibetan closed his eyes, and recited:

> From the minute you come into this world of
>   being
> A ladder is placed in front of you
> To help you climb out of it.

First you were a metal, then you became a plant,
Then you became an animal . . .
Then, marvelously, you became Man, richly
        gifted
With consciousness and reason and faith;
Consider this body dragged out of the dust—
What perfection it has acquired.
When you will have transcended the condition
        of man
You will become—there is no doubt of this—an
        angel,
You will have finished with the earth; your
        house will be heaven.

"The words of Rumi, the Persian Sufi," Blue-Eyes said.
"One of the greatest lovers of man . . . 'And when you
will have transcended the condition of man / You *will*
become—*there is no doubt of this*—an angel.' Rumi is certain that man will transcend his present condition. He
has seen into the future; he knows, as the Buddha knew
and Christ knew, that man's destiny is to be angelic. Are
you following?"

"My dear friend, I'm having the time of my life. I'm
longing to grow wings."

"Rumi does not end there," Blue-Eyes said severely.
"Rumi does not end anywhere. That is the point. Rumi
has a vision of man that *has no end.*"

"Don't shout," I said gently. "I'm sitting next to you."

"I get so fervent sometimes," the Tibetan said. "Rumi
goes on:

        'You will transcend even the condition of an
                angel,
        You will and you must

Dive into the sea
So that your drop of water may become
     a sea . . .'

"There is no end to what man can know, no end to what he can be, no end to how deeply he can dive into the Ocean of God, because that Ocean has no end."

"I shall take your word for it," I couldn't help saying.

Surprisingly, he laughed. "I like you," he said. He paused and crossed his arms. "But Rumi, saint and philosopher though he was, is not entirely right. Man does not need to transcend the earth, leave it behind. He does not need to despise matter, his own hands and feet and penis."

"I have never despised my penis. I've had a very affectionate relationship with my penis, shot through with moments of tremendous sentimental gratitude."

"My dear friend," he said gravely, "we are not here to talk about your relationship with your penis."

Then, I'm afraid to say, he laughed again. I don't think Blue-Eyes quite knew what he was getting into when he chose to lead me onto the higher planes of consciousness.

"My dear friend," he said, wiping his eyes, "promise me you will be quiet for the next few minutes.

"Marx was right to believe that history was tending to the transformation of man, but wrong to ignore the role of the mystical, spiritual sides and needs of man. Rumi was a thousand times right to believe that man's end was self-transcendence, the passing from one state of consciousness to another, but wrong to ignore the role of matter in the process, of the earth, the body." He paused. "The Life Divine is to be lived here on the earth, in the body, not elsewhere. Man is to become God, not in some otherworldly embrace with the Divine, but here on this earth in the body. For thousands of years sages in the East have wanted to call down a light into matter, a divine power that could transfigure it from within. They worked in secret, far from other places of religious thought; they worked in silence, fearing persecution for their beliefs and an end to their labor. This long labor has succeeded. The Light has entered history; it is here, it is working in everything: everything is seething in its grip.

"This Light is burning away all old theories, beliefs, comforts, so its presence will finally be recognized, so man will finally be left with nothing but it, face to face with it, and so with himself.

"Kali-Yuga is both a time of chaos and the time when the Golden Age is born. But the Golden Age to come will be different from any other: no cyclical return, as in the legends, to a place of static perfection, but an entry into new, unsuspected power and radiance, a leap beyond all previous turnings of the wheel into a new being. Look at Kali-Yuga from one side and you see the face of the Black Kali, whose feet dance out the destruction of millions; the bringer of the hydrogen and neutron bombs, and the hundred thousand instruments of torture. Look at Kali-Yuga from the other side and you see the face of the Golden Kali, the Mother, the divine mother who is using this destruction to bring man to a new birth and so to a new manhood, who, with heavenly cruelty, is fashioning man to a new dignity, power, glory, and wisdom. We have been looking too long at the face of the Black Kali; it is time to see behind that face the face of the Golden Mother! Ask the Light to show you the way of its workings, to light up the astonishing paradoxes of its path . . . What I have come to tell you is this: the Light is here now; it has been here for about forty years; and its power is growing."

"I understand hardly anything," I said, "but what I understand least of all is why you are telling me."

"I will explain when I am ready." He walked to the window. "It has always been the case, so our tradition runs, that in Kali-Yuga the chances of salvation are especially strong. In *this* Kali-Yuga something even more astonishing has happened. Not only has the Light entered history, but the highest divine powers are here on earth to help bring it to birth." He spread his arms, and bliss flooded his face. "The Mother is here. The Mother is on the earth. The Golden Mother is with us."

I wanted to laugh, pondy—yes, I wanted to really, to laugh out loud, sardonically, angrily—but as I tried to, as I even began to, *something ran through me.*

When I say "ran through me," I mean it literally. I felt as if I had been run through by a spear of fire. I was in agony. I fell to the floor, screaming. I have had pain in my life, but never a pain like that. It invaded every cell of my body, every bone, every part of every bone. I howled.

Then, as suddenly as the pain had invaded me, it abandoned me. It was replaced by a soft burning, a calm, quiet, assuaging burning, as blissful as the pain had been fierce.

I looked at my hands, my feet. They were glowing, and as they glowed they were changing. How will I, how can I, describe this? They were becoming a different sort of substance, a substance much more fluid, plastic, luminous, than what we call flesh and bone, more like waves than skin, and yet "solid," if that is the right word. No, not solid; closer to water than to earth, but not watery either. The *new* substance, pondy, the *new* body—the body that will house the Light and *be* it.

And as I looked at my hands and feet, I saw around me for the smallest part of a second a crowd of figures, all made of the same substance but far, far more completely—angelic bodies, yet very substantial, more vibrantly present than my sofa, or the Buddhas, or Blue-Eyes. They did not seem to *move,* these bodies; they *glided,* they *flowed* like streams. If to say they were like snakes were not to bring up all sorts of odd connotations, that is how I would describe these beings. And they were beautiful, with a glowing tender opulent shimmering beauty no human words could begin to describe.

I came to. The Tibetan was sitting on the floor with my head in his lap. "Why did you want to laugh?" he asked.

I put my hand up to his mouth. "Please don't speak for a while." I lay on the sofa and he hummed to me and rubbed my temples.

Then he said, "Allow your mind to go to the brink of sleep and then stay there, without going over."

I obeyed.

"Can you hear me?"

His voice sounded at once very far and very close.

"You have been told these things to be of use to those closest to you. You have been granted the grace of helping those you love most. In your dying, my friend, your love has found its purpose. Those whom you love are going on journeys, journeys towards the truth I have revealed. You have been together for many lives, in many different cultures, and now, in this one, at this time, you are each approaching your desire. If I knew the end of your destinies I would tell you, but I do not. Some things are known only by the Divine. All over the earth, small bands of people are receiving the news of the new Light; you are not unique, nor by any means the most advanced. Do not have any of the pride of an élite or of a privileged band. The slightest vanity will make you more vulnerable than you are already. Purify your hearts. Remember that when you work for Her, it is not *you* who work, but She who works through you."

"Will I, my dear friend, ever *see* Her?"

"I do not know. I cannot say."

Then I fell asleep. When I awoke, he had gone.

So there you have it, part of the whole story.

When it was all over, I went out. I hadn't been out in weeks. I went and walked in the night, down the rue Bonaparte to the Seine. All the faces I saw seemed harried, exhausted. A crowd outside Les Deux Magots was watching a clown doing Charlie Chaplin, so badly that I wanted to kick him. Was this the world that was going to be the place of the Divine Life? Were these the people who were going to have in future lives those lissom gleaming bodies? It seemed almost impossible to believe, the maddest of dreams.

Down by the Seine I saw a fat old female drunk being sick into a brown paper bag and then crawling under a stone bench to sleep. I went up to her and tucked some money in the top of her filthy blouse. I stood a long time looking down at her face—her sagging weary face, with its web of blotched blood vessels, the tufts of ugly hair sticking out of her ears.

I heard the Tibetan say, "You must believe that what I said is possible, even in the face of this."

"I believe," I said, out loud. I have never felt so foolish or so happy. I thought of you looking at me asleep and seeing me tired and fat and ill and worn out and being asked by your inner voice, "In the face of this seedy half-crazed old fag, can you believe?" and I prayed to Her for you to have the chutzpah to say yes.

Wondergran

P.S. Now read Anna's letter. She is nearing the fire too.
P.P.S. I didn't give the old drunk *that* much money. Proportion in all things.
P.P.P.S. When I get even holier I'm going to go down and give Odile de Valois a vision myself.
P.P.P.P.S. What do you think all this has to do with those wacky entries in Richard's notebooks? I've been so wrapped up in myself (oh the transcending ego!) I'd forgotten about him. Did he see Her? Who is She? Where is She?

·THREE·

Benares

Adolphe and Charles,

You have been wondering, I know, why I haven't written. Almost immediately after coming to India I fell ill. I had three quiet days in Delhi. Then I went to Benares and got sick. For a week I was in delirium, lying in a dirty bed in a small empty dingy hotel near the Burning Ghats; I had a temperature of a hundred and three for four days running. I nearly died. I have only just recovered my strength to understand what has been happening to me.

I hate writing letters. I sit upright at the desk staring at the white paper and feeling as if I were back at convent school. "Anna, can't you write any better than that?" "I will try, Sister Mary." "Trying is not enough, Anna. We can do nothing by our own efforts. It is the Virgin who will write from within you." "I hope so, Sister Mary." How lucky to have been to convent school in the north of England! Nothing ever seems quite so grisly afterwards. Not even dying in Benares.

Don't you dare, Charles, write a story called "Dying in Benares."

I arrived in Delhi in the early morning in a state of

euphoria. Nothing is less conducive to ecstasy than Palam airport—even walking down the Air India ramps seems an act of courage, and the shabbiness of the airport, the leering insistence of the customs officers (walking around with their walkie-talkies as if they had just discovered them) ruffling through all my lingerie with a more than professional passion, would have dampened any enthusiasm less than mine. Yet just to smell early-morning India off the tarmac—smoke from the fires of those who live nearby, the indefinable smell of the Indian morning, so wide, so vast and fresh—started me off. The woman in front of me had woven jasmine into her hair. Fat though she was, and in one of those flower-splattered nylon saris, she walked with the aromatic, lightly swinging grace only Indian women have. If I didn't dislike the pope so much I'd have got down and kissed the earth.

When I think how frivolous and arrogant I was when I last came to India (I can still hear my voice shouting at a porter in Bangalore station, "Pick that fucking thing up!"—when the man was so tired and thin he could hardly walk), I tremble at myself. Now I have not come to India to "rest" or "recuperate," I have come . . . Why have I come? I have come to ask India to help me. I have come to ask the jasmine and the jacaranda and the smell of the morning and the peace that is still here (god knows how) and the sound of the bicycle bells in the bazaar tingling with the smell of hot sweets and shit and steaming tea to *help* me. I am nearly forty; I have no man, no child; I have done very little (writing a few songs for the idle rich to sing does not count); I have wasted myself on people who did not love me enough and who were not worth the chaotic feeling I wasted on them. I am asking India's help for the rest of my life.

Of course I realize how stupid it is to write "I am asking India to help me," stupid and presumptuous. But let it stand. It is the truth.

Those first three days! I hardly slept. I didn't look up anyone I knew in Delhi. I booked into the Ambassador Hotel and walked. I walked up and down the banks of the Jumuna in old Delhi. The river was a sort of holy-men ash white, frothing slightly at its banks. The sand of its banks looks like the accumulation of centuries of bone, bones worn thin by the water. I walked up Alipur Road to the Old Secretariat and into the park they are making there; sitting at dusk in an old tomb, I was surrounded suddenly by peacocks, who danced for me. Danced! Imagine that. Anna in black, without makeup, surrounded by peacocks, their tails spread as far open as they could possibly be, strutting, all their brilliant colors deeper in that late gold-dust light. I've never had so many males excited by me at once! I sat in a café in Chandi Chowk all morning just looking, watching India walk past. Everything is out there, everything, the dead, the dying, the mad, the clowns, the rich—they are all there in the open—the rich men with their shining new American cars and their silver cigarette holders, the poor with their thin blankets, coming in for a tea after a night under the bridges over the road or in the rotting arches of the station. I saw a madman crouching in a series of puddles and an old woman following behind him patiently, trying to put food into his hands; as I was about to leave the teahouse, a funeral procession came past. The reek of the garlands of marigolds and the sweating, half-naked, skinny bodies carrying the bier are still with me.

I became an eye in those days, a vast transparent eye; I forgot myself in the misery and splash and scent and noise around me; I found myself, like the light, touching everything—the rings in the women's noses, the sun-blackened backs of the coolies, the fly-covered tops of the tables, everything—with fresh grace and recognition. I even conquered my fear of street food, and ate fistfuls of samosas—probably, god knows, stuffed with dog meat.

One morning, looking for the sculpture museum, I ended up in the arcades of Rashtrapati Bhavan, watching a group of women practicing their folk dances for the parade in January. It was about midday, and they shared their food with me, feeling me all over, showing me their skirts and jewels and how to braid my hair their way. How delicious that food tasted, those chapatis and curried potatoes, sitting there on the grass with those women. And their dances! So wild and graceful at the same time. One of the women understood my broken Hindi, and explained that she was a grandmother. She looked younger than me. She said her husband was a laborer and earned little, and drank, and was much older than her, and sick. But that was life, she added. Her gaiety made me feel ashamed.

Western photographers come and shoot "the misery of India." Why do they never dare to shoot (dreadful word!) "the happiness of India"? Wouldn't sell, I suppose. Wouldn't confirm the West in its uneasy wretched vanity, its belief that money makes you sing, honey. Could be a line from one of my old songs, couldn't it? Oh, the things one has done for money. The things I have done for money. The songs, the trips to Mauritius with fat old aristos with tastes in *partouzes*, the dinner parties sat through in the hope of an invitation to the dinner of the friend of a friend of a Contact. What absurdity it all seems here.

Don't think I don't also see and feel the horror here. My first night in Delhi, I saw—just outside the Ambassador Hotel—a dog with its back broken, dying in a ditch. I ran to the doorman, I begged him to get someone. He looked at me as if I were mad. I wanted to kill the dog myself, but didn't have the guts . . . The horror is easy to see, easy, even, to react to, to despise or to pity. What is harder is to see the wholeness, the health that survives within it, despite and beyond it. Despite the Sikh killings, despite the burning of the young wives, the ill-treatment of the untouchables, the corrupt politicians and the quack doctors, the whole vast edifice of misery. How to explain that? On the train to Benares, an old retired banker with a handlebar moustache and a slow Cambridge voice said, "God lives in India because we need him so much. He needs to be needed." "How do you know he is a he?" I said, and his face brightened. "I am myself a devotee of Kali. For Kali is the goddess of India—who else could express the terror and the beauty of this, my land?" And he began to hum something, very shakily:

> Mother of love and destruction,
> Even pain is beautiful at your hands,
> Even terror is a gift if you give it.

We were crossing a bridge over the Ganges at the time, and the banker opened his hands in adoration and closed his eyes. Everyone in the carriage shut their eyes and seemed to pray for a moment. It is healing to be in a country where God is remembered in the fields, in trains, by the side of the road peeling a banana. It is healing to be reminded everywhere that behind *this* life there is another, woven into it, coexisting with it, continually flooding it. Time is so stretched out here that it at moments becomes transparent, a thin gauze you can see through.

It can be frightening, that long lazy stretching-out. (I panic sometimes—will the train never come? Will I always be sitting here on the ground with the smell of urine in my nostrils?) So much in myself is revealed to me when I no longer have my friends to ring up, my songs to write, my stupid dinners to distract myself with—so much regret, pain, hollowness. Yet when the panic and unease subside, it happens. My attachment to the past, to "Anna," dissolves, and I am here, in the compartment or the café—or here, looking into the eye of the lizard looking at me, hoping it will not move—or here, seeing the lizard dart up, up into the brown shadows near the fan . . .

The things I cannot help feeling self-pitying about in Paris—that I have no man, that I have no child, that I am nearly forty—here seem so irrelevant. I find an Anna I have neglected, mocked, abandoned, been scared of for so long. How difficult it is in our world, where everyone is running, to dare to discover that standing still is sufficient, more than sufficient, rich, the richest thing of all. I know I should be strong enough to feel this in the West, surrounded by all the familiar sights and faces. But I am not. If ever I am, it will be India that has helped me. I shall be made strong by this earth, these smells, the patience in the faces of these people who have known so much suffering and have not lost their dignity or their sense of some starry order, some cool and soaring constellation of truth that, if it explains nothing, rings all that is with its power, bathes all that is in its light.

I realize I have been writing for two hours and not talked about dying in Benares yet. Benares, then.

I sit and think, "How will I explain it to them—my illness, its terror, what I learnt . . ." and as I think, I hear Benares out there. I am in this small crumbling room with paper-thin walls and brown shadows. There is a cracked mirror above a small chest of drawers (mahogany, turn-of-the-century, British). There is a large cracked white jug full of water dirty enough to have come from the Ganges. And the window, which has one pane of glass missing, opens out onto a small back alley that two hundred years down itself opens onto the river. Sometimes I think I can hear the river. I want to so badly, I think I invent its lapping, out there, on the rim of hearing. I can smell it, though. Not a rancid smell, surprisingly—but very rich, watery, a smell full of ash and mud . . .

I have no idea why I came to Benares in the first place. Three days in Delhi, and then, *poof,* I caught the train to Benares. I was surprised at myself. I had planned to begin a long slow trek south, to Bangalore and the Baba Ashram. But all of a sudden I found myself saying, "Benares. That is where I must go next." Someone once told me in Paris (not *all* dinner parties are wasted) that Jung hated Benares, hated its promiscuous mix of gold and God, corruption and holiness. I think I must have decided then that I had to come.

> Love has pitched his mansion in
> The place of excrement;

Nothing can be sole or whole
That has not first been rent.

Remember shouting out those lines, Charles, late one New Year's Eve, weaving down the rue de Seine? I hope you've improved your stage Irish accent.

I arrived in Benares late at night. The train was eight hours late. What lunacy at the station! Row after row of snoring beggars, sweepers half asleep on their brooms, pretending to work but missing all the piles of peels and paper. No one to tell you anything or help. I felt as if I had arrived at the gates of hell. Even the clocks were wrong. They looked solid, Western, old British, with comforting hands and warm russet stains from the rain and moisture on their white. But no two said the same time. For some it was three, some five, some eleven. No one bothered to correct them or seemed to know which, if any, might be accurate. I tried to talk to three men who looked like station masters; they had the semblances of uniforms, at any rate. "Is there a bus into the city?" Smile. "Do the buses leave at this hour?" Larger smile, showing several black teeth. "Is there a station hotel?" Slightly shrunken smile, a lowering of the eyelids as if one had said something obscene ... I started screaming incoherently and waving my hands about. Patient, uncomprehending, slightly scared smile. Just in time I stopped and began to laugh. "Oh, my god," I said to myself, "now I have *really* arrived. Delhi was the pâté de foie gras. This is the entrée." I sat down on my little black trunk (how I love my trunk, with its labels and its scratches!) and I read one of the four books I have brought—*Alice in Wonderland*. I recommend Benares railway station in the middle of the night in a state of

famished hysteria as the ideal place to read Lewis Car-
roll. We'll do it together one day. But you have to have
had a day-long train journey first. Otherwise your mind
isn't frayed enough to be illuminated. Nothing can be
sole or whole . . .

After a good hour of reading I felt calmed. I strolled
out of the station entrance, and as if by miracle a taxi, a
shiny new yellow taxi, rolled up. Its driver was about
eighty, with shaky hands and a nicotine-stained moustache. "My younger brother very good man. Keep very
clean hotel. Very close to holy river." "Okay," I said. "*Teek
hai.* Just get me there and I will pray for you for the rest
of my life."

I think my illness, whatever it was, started on that
journey. I remember feeling feverish, slightly, but I ignored it—looking out, drinking in the city at night.
Once we were passing an alley and I looked down it and
saw the river gleaming in the moonlight, only, what,
thirty yards away. My heart leapt and I thought, "It was
worth it for that—for that glimpse."

I booked into the hotel, where I have stayed on despite
everything (and I mean despite everything—the noise,
the cockroaches, the manager's sickly smile, his tepid
lemon juice). I have stayed on because, as I discovered
that night and have told you, it is near the river. That
river. To be near the river so that it can flow through
your dreams . . . That first night, however, I could not
sleep. I was far too tired. So I walked. I walked on and
on, in circles, baffled and delighted and exhausted until
at last, almost when I had given up, I *did* come to the
river. (Since then, I have found it is very close. I am glad
I had to wander then. I feel as if I earned it in some way,
stepping into all those cowpats.) Dawn was beginning.

The river was calm, wide, silvery in the early light. I could almost see the individual threads. It was being woven, rhythmically, in one of those complex interwoven rhythms that Indian music has mastered so well, rhythms that almost escape us, they are so subtle and fast.

Bells rang out from all over the city. I found myself quickly surrounded by people of all ages and sizes, coming to worship in the river. I cannot imagine anyone not being at least for a moment silenced by the sight of the Ganges at dawn and the thousands bathing in it, calmly, naturally, without any false piety. I stepped back and sat by a tree to the side. An old woman bathing close to me saw me watching her. She came out of the river, her sari clinging to her and her hands cupping some water, and walked over to me, dripping river water along the gray worn stones of the steps. Gently she marked my forehead with the water, and without saying anything walked on. I have tried to picture her face many times, but I cannot. All I remember of her is her eyes—very wide and burning—and the orange dot in the middle of her forehead.

The illness began a few hours later. I refer to it as "the illness" not out of some sacred Indo-Gangetic awe (rest assured), but because none of the doctors that the manager—after some fairly heavy bribery—summoned to my bedside could make up their minds what it was. One said hepatitis, which it couldn't have been, as I feel all rightish now, although god knows I did pee orange, and felt so weak that I fell down every time I stood up, like a drunk in a pantomime (and on my face too, several times, which has added an interesting patchwork of bruises to my cheeks). Another said, with Dickensian relish, "Madam, I regret to inform you that you have acquired"—*acquired!* What a delicious euphemism!— "dengue fever." And sure enough, my bones were shaking, my temperature was high, etc., etc., all of which are signs of dengue (and there was a small epidemic of it in Delhi, where I had just been). One of the waiters at the Ambassador had it. The doctor added, "Memsahib, it can on occasion be fateful." *Fateful?* He was right, the old boy with the glasses stuck on discreetly with tape, he was right . . .

One thing I discovered was that descriptions in Victorian novels of "bone-shaking fevers" are not poetic. Your bones do shake. The fever I had went right into and along the marrow. Sometimes I had only the strength to whimper with pain. There were days when my whole mind was pain, nothing but pain, pain burning along and in every bone. Some days I was so weak I could not even turn over; I had to lie there gazing up at the labyrinth of cracks in the ceiling. I begged the manager to change my bedclothes every day, but some days I was just forgotten and lay there in my sweat, every bone aching, unable to move. I ate nothing for five days and am now thinner than I have been since I was at school—I look down at my wrists and am afraid of bending them too fast in case they should snap. I look at my chest in the bath and see each bone in my ribcage distinctly. My breasts seem to me two small hanging rags.

I do not want to be morbid and I haven't described to you "what I went through" so as to ask your sympathy. I just want you to know. There are many ways in which I think the illness a blessing. How Sister Mary would love that! "Ah, at last, Anna, you have bent your wild and rebellious will to the ways of the Lord." And Sister

Agnes would fold her hands piously and say, "The ways of the Lord God are beyond our ken. Drink up your Bovril." And Mother Superior, exalted from Dubonnet: "Ah, my dear, sometimes we are weak enough to enter heaven." But it was a blessing, it was, and not so differently from the way the nuns would have meant (there was, thank god, no Bovril). Not a blessing. Such a scented, pansy word. A gift, a ruthless gift, the kind that makes you aware of what you are *not* giving.

I think I fell ill from a wish to die—not really to die; the thought of suicide has cheered me up so often in my life I wouldn't actually do it—but to die to the old Anna. I came to India to die. Why else come now, at this time in my life? Oh, I should be having those vitamin shots Odile told me about, at the sides of my eyelids, to take away their sag; I should be doing aerobics in some center in Montmartre. I should be "getting into films," like every other aging half-beauty in Paris. But those are the games of the old Anna, games she never played very well and despised herself for playing at all. Games that bored her not at the end but very near the beginning, and which she played out of boredom and misery and FEAR, oh mostly FEAR. I think FEAR should always have capital letters. I came to India to die to myself. I thought India would be powerful enough to kill Anna off, violent and beautiful enough to *do it,* to do it as no lover has ever done . . . And although I cannot claim to be dead (the health of the Anna ego must be obvious from these pages), I have had a taste of what this kind of dying might be like, and have been alternately terrified and exalted and calmed.

I hear the river now quite distinctly. It is a windy day and the water is lapping against the stone steps. I wish we could go down now and take boat together and wander choppily down it, with the wind in our faces, carrying away the words that are inessential, that do not reach. The bodies floating and decomposing around us would make us very accurate.

It was on the third day that I became conscious of what was happening to me. Up till then I had been suffering, just suffering, groaning and retching and pissing orange. I realized on the third day that the pain might go on a long time and that I would have to make friends with it. Yes, make friends with it. Not treat it as alien, but as part of my body, part of my *life*. Not to be rejected, hated, despised, but to be approached with sympathy. Perhaps in pain there is something wanting to be released, to be liberated. The doctors offered me drugs, but I refused them. Not from courage, but from a desire for relationship. Can you understand? I don't want to be drugged anymore. I've been drugged so long, I'd rather suffer atrociously than be numb ever again.

When I accepted the pain, it changed. It did not go away; it was at times unbearable. I was not ashamed to howl. I thought, "In Benares you can howl. No one has to pretend here. Two hundred yards away, the priests are hitting corpses as they sit up in the fire. Crack, crack, the spine breaks. In the city of death you are allowed to howl." I howled. But I also heard myself howling. I watched myself turning and twisting and heard myself screaming and became slowly but more completely detached from what I was suffering. There was Anna on the bed, lost in pain; there was "I" or "Whoever" (I like "Whoever") a little above Anna on the bed, free from her, unclaimed by her, able to watch her with compassion, to float above her. Every day, however, Whoever became a little more free, a little more serene. This detachment was not indifference; I cared for myself with a clear tenderness, saying "Don't think like that, it will not help," or "Turn over now," or "Try to keep your breathing even," almost like a gym mistress or Sister Agnes. Can you understand? And from experience I learnt a little not to fear death at all. I discovered that I have never essentially feared death. Perhaps we *learn* to fear death. Perhaps as children we are in some unity with it, which is later robbed from us. We become adults, anxious for our lives and so fearful of death.

The person I discovered and released on that bed was not anxious for life, though very solicitous of it, and so not at all afraid to look into the face of death. There were moments when I knew I was on the brink of death, and if I had chosen to die I could have rolled over that edge. It was very important at those moments to decide. To *decide*, not against death, but for the new life that was beginning after this meeting with death, a life that would always have this meeting under it as a promise, a reminder, an inspiration.

I decided to live. I decided to live to begin to give birth in this life to the person I uncovered in my meeting with death, the person in me that rose to meet death without fear. That is the real reason for going on living—to experience life through the eyes and feelings of *this* person, whose vision is free and unanxious. Perhaps it was to meet this person that I was deprived for so long of everything I thought I wanted—a husband, children, material security. It was to meet her or him or it (all three together) that I came to Benares. If I had been given what I thought I wanted, I would have lived ignorant of this. I do not feel grateful for my confused sad stupid past—to be grateful would be ridiculous. I feel it was necessary and is now over.

You can tell from this letter I am still myself, still struggling with old ghosts, still talking back to old torturers. But I hope you can tell too that I am also moving crablike into something different. During the illness, I even began to see Peter, my dreadful ex, differently. At last. For years I was too hurt even to think of him. You know the crap he pulled—the lies, the confidence tricks, the making me think of him as the Great Artist and not see him for weeks because (so he said) he was *working* (in fact he was screwing everything that walked). Yes. All of that is true. But it was also because of him that I first came to India. It was because of him that I began to read the Gita and Rumi and the Dhammapada (come to think of it, Charles, didn't you first discover the Dhammapada through him?). I realize now how much of my naiveté was responsible for his lies. If I had been cannier, he could not have dared to get away with so much. And if I hadn't been so in love with Art (Capital *A*), he would never have been able to use Art as a net to snare me in. If I had worked at realizing my creativity (I began to write songs after our divorce) instead of wanting to be the muse, instead of wanting him to live that part of myself for me, perhaps he wouldn't have needed to pretend so much, to flee me so often. I forced him to be *great,* or try to be. He was terrified of being mediocre. I see now that my desire for him to be transcendent drove him away from me and must have made him suffer and hate me. Why has it taken me so long to face all this? I realize too that if he was often violent with me—hitting me, throwing me across the room, once even breaking my arm (how calmly I write that now)—it was at least

149

partly because my possessiveness, my psychological hunger for him, was as violent as his desperation. I want to see him again. I want to have one last chance to explain, to apologize. To try to see him clearly. If only for an hour in a bus station or a café. Will life be that generous? I doubt it. But the fact that I have begun to release him inwardly from all the rage and guilt I have heaped on his head all these years releases me, helps me to breathe.

This is by far the longest letter I have written in my life. I have written it wildly, as it came, because I wanted to give you myself, what I am thinking. Not just to sort out and arrange. All that seems petty. It is not neatness I want. I've been so neat. Remember, Charles, how I arranged everything in the refrigerator, in neat little rows . . . And how I shouted at you when you didn't change your shirt. Be as dirty as much as you like. You can even wear those red shirts I hate. I renounce Anna the arranger, Anna the boss, Anna the vampire. She was a selfish frightened mean-souled bitch. (Any protests? Speak up! I want a *few* protests!) If that Anna reappears, please, whatever she does, *take an ax to her.* She may call the police, she may call you all the names she can; go on hacking . . .

During the illness I did, believe it or not, think about you two. I know it seems as if I would have had very little time to think of anything but myself (selves), what with the floatings and the writhings and the inquisitions. But you were always there with me, by my side, helping me. You especially, Adolphe. I felt so much for you, Adolphe—so much for what you are now enduring . . . I find I love you intensely. Wipe that grin off your face.

And you, Charles, I see more clearly than I have ever done. I see your vanity, your evasiveness, your priggishness, your cult of suffering, your *maleness,* all these, more sharply than ever, and in more tender perspective than I can describe.

And us three together? That is a mystery, perhaps the mystery of our lives. Lying in bed, I thought a great deal about that . . . the crystal we seem to make, each turning as the other turns, each catching a different glint of the same light . . . Why are we together? Why have we fused so? Partly it is the solitude each of us knows that links us. My childlessness, your homosexuality, our peculiar intelligences, worldly and spiritually hungry at the same time, our peculiar mixture of vanity and humility—each composes a solitude, intense and troubling. And that links us, makes us understand each other's jokes, each other's silences.

But there is another reason, I think. One that cannot be defined—and I don't really want to. It is a higher reason, and my coming to India and undergoing all that I have described is very much part of this. Your dying, Adolphe, and Charles, your going to find Richard—these too are parts of this. I feel that a design is unfolding. That's not just because I'm better and have just had my first gin since I came to India. Gin and lemon juice: the infamous nimboo pani, drink of memsahibs with riding crops . . .

It will be difficult to write to me. Why don't you send me photocopies of the letters *you* have been exchanging, as well as fresh separate ones to me, to the Baba Ashram, Bangalore? I'm going there tomorrow, or the next day. Sweeping down the center of India on one of those interminable train journeys I love more than anything. Every time I smell fresh chapatis I will wish you the smell also; every time I see out of the window a dog asleep under a tree, or a river in the dawn, or a man scrubbing a cow's back, I shall see it for you, and with you. I will also send you the flies, the smell of the station lavatories, the wens, the scarred feet, the goats' blood on the statues of Kali, for perspective's sake.

Always
Anna

Underneath Anna's signature Adolphe wrote:

"I'm sending copies of all our letters to A at the ashram as requested.

"I always thought the husband rather dishy, from the photos. Rather regretted that he was out in the cold.

"Don't think I—or we—have finished with the Tibetan. Lots more golden eggs from *that* goose, I can assure you. Be patient. All in God's time."

CHARLES TO ADOLPHE

New York

After your letter and Anna's I frankly feel like hitchhiking to Maine and lying on a rock for the rest of my life.

Evolutionary visions, Tibetans coming and vanishing, dying in Benares—*dio mio,* it's more than a body can stand.

I'm amazed; I'm taking it all in slowly. Anna's letter is such a grave delight I have read it already four or five times.

Something strengthening happened this morning after I had finished reading your letters. All their excitement made me hungry, so I walked across the park to the Opera Espresso in Lincoln Center. It's a dingy place with bad food, but it is full of memories for me. Richard and I used to go there before performances at the Met. (That was the time of my campaign to initiate Richard into opera. I thought that if he understood the extravagances of opera, he would understand my excesses. Alas. He preferred *Porgy and Bess* to *Tristan,* and bloody Vivaldi to both.) I ate some blueberry pie; dreamed of Anna in Benares; tried to picture what the New Men you saw must have looked like (*very* unlike the fat sad women sitting there, the men with heavy work-pouches under their eyes); transported myself first to Paris and your room, and then to India—not to Benares, because I have never been there, but to Mathura, where I first saw the Ganges. Sitting there, I felt soaked in Anna's letter and in my memories of India.

I walked out of the Opera Espresso. Someone tapped me on the shoulder. I turned round to see . . . *two Indians.* One about fifty, spry, obviously Tamil (those heavy features), with bloodshot eyes and a watchchain rather comically dangling from his right jacket pocket. The other in his early twenties, small, perfectly shaped, with the tiny jeweled features of a Keralan and the beginnings of a moustache. The older man said, "Good sir, please be so very kind as to tell us the nearest subway."

We fell into conversation. The Indians produced notebooks, cards, bits of paper, and wrote down all their addresses. They were on holiday in New York from Kuwait. ("Please, dear sir, not to come to Kuwait. Very bad place. No girls. No nothing. Sleep, then work, then house, then sleep.") We had only ten minutes together; by the end of that, I knew that the older man was "the father of four, dear sir," that the younger was called Mustapha, was branch manager of a building company, liked Bruce Springsteen, had a younger sister who was marriageable and a brother who worked in Malaysia. Adolphe, imagine it: reading Anna's letter and then meeting them, in that particular way, in the middle of a gray New York winter morning. We parted on the subway steps, salaaming and bowing.

You know I told you once of the experience I had at Mahabalipuram—when I danced naked in the lightning (!)—you must remember, you laughed. Well, Adolphe, the older man came from there.

I went back to the Opera Espresso. I needed another coffee. I remembered another experience at Mahabalipuram that I haven't told you about. I had forgotten it, in fact, till this morning.

The experience was a simple one. I heard the sound the mystics talked of, the *shabd,* the great wind-sound of creation. I was walking on the beach back to my hotel and I heard it. It was not the sound of the sea. It was a vast soft roaring humming (I can't describe it any other way), in which every other sound was being born continually. I was quite clear about what I was hearing. I had spent the evening in the shore temple and had prayed to Shiva to give me a sign of his power. I stood on the beach for about an hour, and the sound was all about me, swirling and pulsing. It is, I have since been told, a very minor experience, one that beginners have. What a beginning! To hear that power, that sound that you know is the hum that supernovas make as they spin in space . . . Anything is possible to the power. Anything. Even the birthing of the new creatures you saw.

I heard that sound again in the Opera Espresso this morning. Ha! One can hear it anywhere. With the clink of coffee cups, the very unsoft roar of the traffic outside, people jabbering about real estate at the next table. If you can hear the *shabd* in the Opera Espresso (this is you talking), you can hear it anywhere.

"Aren't you ever going to leave?" said the waitress with the goiter. "This isn't a hotel, you know." Then the sound did end. A Brooklyn rasp is very powerful.

Your letters, the Indians, the sound—that was my morning. It made me strong.

I needed all the strength I could get because I went to lunch with Richard's father. Not at a restaurant, but in the large, white, mostly empty loft on East Thirteenth and Second.

I did not want to meet Richard's father. Everything that I had heard about him from Richard made me certain I would dislike him. In Richard's version of the family melodrama he was the *pater annihilans*, the philanderer who sacrificed everyone's happiness to his whims, the spoiled ne'er-do-well who stumbled from one futile fantastical scheme to another (one year it would be championship sailing, the next computers, the next learning Japanese in two months, to start an East–West fashion business).

Richard (of course) was obsessed with his father. He longed for his father's approval and feared his jealousy. "My father," he used to say, "hates me because I am as handsome as he was, because my mother loves me, because I always beat him at chess, and because I am living the life he would have liked to live but never dared to." This was a speech I heard often. At the same time as Richard mocked his father, patronized him, heaped on his head all the misery of his adolescence, and noted

155

grimly every detail of his father's latest failure ("There is the enthusiastic stage, followed by the absurd stage, followed by the mendacious stage"), he also talked, often, dreamily, almost incestuously, of his father's beauty, his green eyes, his strong arms and shoulders, the way that men and women stared at him when he strolled into a room.

Naturally I was jealous of Richard's father, whom naturally I was not allowed to meet. I felt judged in comparison with this brawny forty-five-year-old who ran every morning half naked through the woods and boxed to near-professional standards—judged and found puny, effete, European, all right for reading Yeats aloud and talking about Rembrandt, but not the real thing, the real male McCoy. So in revenge I imagined Father as a spoiled WASP lout who would wear studiedly casual *Gentleman's Quarterly* clothes, have Richard's vanity and posturing but none of his poetry, and hate intellectuals and fags.

The man who opened the door four stories up was so different from any picture I had formed of him that I almost cried out.

He was thin and limping. One half of his body was clearly paralyzed. The simple black sweater he was wearing hung loosely on him.

Then I remembered—Richard's father had had a stroke last year. How could I have forgotten that? How could I have been so obsessed with my own images as to have forgotten that? He had had a stroke while out sailing, and had almost drowned.

The father extended his one usable hand—his left—and smiled. The famous green eyes were shrewder than I had anticipated. There was no imperiousness in them, or mockery; only a curiosity, a detached interest. He

156

spoke slowly and precisely. He had clearly had to fight hard to regain the power of speech.

"It is good of you to have come."

Christ, I thought, this man is going to *charm* me.

The loft was almost entirely empty, except for a long table, a sofa, and some chairs. The bedrooms were off to the left behind a glass door. It looked surprisingly ascetic for the man I had imagined—a simple place, bare, full of light.

Richard's father shambled painfully across the floor and pointed to a chair. He lowered himself gingerly into one opposite, stretching out his paralyzed leg.

"We need a drink," he said, smiling an eerie smile on only one side of his face. "I shouldn't drink because of all the medication I have to take. But I do. I can't give up everything. Perhaps next year I'll be able to give up everything. See that small cupboard over there? The hooch is in there.

"The ice is in the fridge. Notice how silent the fridge is. I looked all over New York for a silent refrigerator. One of life's supreme luxuries."

We clinked glasses.

I saw his arms in the black sweater—how strong they were. Even in this state, he was still a handsome man. His face was finer-boned than I had expected. Perhaps the illness had refined it. It was not the face of a roué or a spendthrift: it had lines of serious grief and bafflement. His hands surprised me. They were very large, with long tapering fingers. If I had not known that he boxed, I would have assumed he played the piano with them.

He caught me staring at him and smiled, with a certain irony.

"Not a pretty sight, I'm afraid," he said. "Remember

that sentence of Swift's, from *Tale of a Tub*? 'Flaying had altered her complexion for the worse.' I'm misquoting, but you get the idea."

He looked at me and put down his glass.

"I was against asking you to come. It was my wife's idea. Strange still to call her my wife, when we have not lived together for nearly twenty years. But we never got divorced. I'm not sure why. Habit. A kind of faith. I don't know. I'm rambling. I spend a great deal of time alone, and you ramble when you live alone."

"I write. I live alone."

"So you understand. I've not been alone often in my life. I've always managed to avoid it. Now I find I like it."

"Why were you against the idea of me coming?"

I had, I realized with a shock, no notion of what he would reply. He paused, looked into his drink.

"I felt this family had caused you enough suffering. I felt we should leave you alone."

It was the last reply I had expected. I stared at him.

He smiled. "Paris must be a wonderful place to work. I used to dream of living there when young, and having a view of the Seine from a small studio window. I didn't know what I would *do* in the studio, of course. I was a vain young man and imagined I could do anything I wanted. It was a fantasy I managed to prolong till last year." He paused. "I have caused a great deal of pain through my weakness, and I am responsible for much of the misery of those I love. But nothing is over finally, is it, until you die? There is time to change. That is perhaps the one thing I have retained that is good—the belief that we can always reinvent life. That belief has wreaked havoc in my life. But now, in this state . . ." He didn't continue, but I knew what he meant. "I suppose you think this very American and optimistic of me."

"Not necessarily. Guilt can be indulgent too."

He sipped his drink.

"My son," he said suddenly. "I have hurt him most of all."

I started to say something.

"No," he cut me short. "I want to talk to you. I want to tell you a story. It may explain some things . . . I have loved three people in my life. My wife. I did love her, for all the pain I caused her. The woman I live with now. I do love her, for all the pain she causes me. And a man. In some ways him most of all. I called Richard after him. Richard does not know the full story. I have never quite had the courage to tell him."

I had no idea what he was talking about. I watched his hands on the table, clasping and unclasping.

"The first Richard—let us call him that—was my English teacher at Choate. He had just graduated from Amherst when he came to teach at the school. I was seventeen, he twenty-two or -three. He was from a wasp banking family in New York, but had a southern mother who came from one of the oldest southern dynasties. He never tired of speaking of her—it was she who had inspired his life, given him the taste for beauty, his sense of style. He wore silk vests and bow ties and smoked cheroots, and held night-long poetry sessions in his rooms. I heard Auden for the first time with him, and Wallace Stevens. He was a fine sportsman too, the best tennis player I have ever known, and I was five years younger than him and the star of the team. That first term we met we would often play the whole afternoon together. He would nearly always win, damn him. 'Hughes,' he would say with a laugh, 'you are not so good as you pretend to be.' He was handsome, in a lithe, blond way. I have never seen more beautiful eyes in any man or woman—not even in my son; they were large with enormous lashes and full of fire. When he read poems to us boys he used to weep if he was moved. Can you imagine what that did to us repressed wasps? Here was a man brave enough to *cry*. His ability at sports, his general manliness, saved him from any suspicions of being effeminate, which would have scared us like hell. We hero-worshiped him, hung on his every word, like schoolgirls. We copied his walk, his way of talking (with a slight drawl), his way of reading aloud (a long pause after every line); we stayed up nights to read the books he insisted 'no man could be called a man' if he had not read."

Mr. Hughes took another long swig at his bourbon. "I spent a lot of time with him, alone. Playing tennis together and talking, we became very close. We would go back to his rooms, shower together, lie on his floor listening to music. He was princely, and I flowered in his warmth and his belief in me. I loved him. The other day I came across letters I wrote to my mother from school, and they are full of nothing but him, what we did together, what he said, the music of all kinds he had given me. I wince at their ignorance now when I read them. But it was the early fifties, Charles. Homosexuality was unthinkable to people of my class and my background. I had perhaps heard the word four or five times. Everyone talked of *fags* or *queers* with complete contempt.

"It never occurred to me that Richard and I were in love. I knew I was attracted to girls and attractive to them. He and I used to hug a lot and touch each other in the ritualistic ways American men can. Once as I was leaving him one evening he kissed me on the cheek. It seemed natural to me, and I kissed him back. Why not? We were *brothers*. Brothers are *allowed* to kiss each other.

"About a week later we were lying on the floor, a little drunk, listening to Billie Holiday, and he took my hand and said, 'I have something to tell you.' And he told me. He told me everything. That he loved me and wanted to sleep with me.

"I behaved badly. I couldn't, I suppose, have done anything else. I was shaking, but I managed the kind of cold defensive speech men are good at. I said that we should stop seeing each other. For *his* sake. The hypocrisy of that, 'for *his* sake.' I even brought up the names of two girls I was writing to. Now I've forgotten their names. He went silent and white. He said, 'Then you had better go.' We shook hands! Can you imagine the lunacy of that? After that, shaking hands . . ."

There was a long silence.

"We did see each other, and we stayed friends. Richard married at twenty-five, a strong intelligent beautiful woman from a wealthy Philadelphia family. He left Choate and went to live in Philadelphia, and wrote several books on the Victorians. Not very good books—he was always more of a talker than a writer—but worthy. He had two children—a daughter, and a son he called after me."

Richard's father paused and looked across at me. "So we kept up appearances, you see . . . To all appearances Richard's life was settled. We saw each other five times a year, on average, and were gentle but cautious with each other. We never talked about what had happened. We talked about books, music, our families. We were each other's best friends. Three years ago he died, of cancer.

161

Once towards the end I was sitting by his bedside. He was asleep, dozing. He woke up, saw me, and gave me this strange, absolutely beautiful smile. 'It doesn't matter,' he said. 'It wasn't the time.' I found myself saying, 'I was not brave enough. I should have given myself to you. I wanted to.' 'I know,' he said, and went to sleep again."

He finished his drink.

"I would have loved women more wisely and less selfishly if I had been able completely to love Richard, and I would have been a better father to my son. But I was scared of loving him too much, of loving anyone that much."

He hung his head as his son had often done; we said nothing. How strange and sad it was to listen to a story so like Richard's and mine . . .

"I expected to find you very different," I said.

"Perhaps I *was* the person you expected to find. A year ago I could not have spoken as I have. Do you love Richard?"

"I have done."

"Did he love you?"

"As far as he could. Farther than he could, sometimes."

"I thought so. He has something of the courage of his mother. Find my son, and love him well."

I smiled. "You said that like a patriarch."

"I am," he said, raising his glass. "A modern patriarch. With a very small, battered *p*."

"Thank god."

"It's time for one last drink. Don't make it too strong or I'll get hell from Mary when she rings. She rings at three thirty, to make sure I'm starting my exercises. I'm determined to straighten this thing out." He pointed to his leg. "It may be good for my soul to be a cripple, but it gets very boring. You must come and meet Mary. She'd like you, but she'd give you hell."

"Why?"

"Mary gives everyone hell. Thinks it's good for them. Comes from living with me for so long, I suppose. When I had the stroke she said, 'Don't whine about it. Face it. Start now.' Women are much stronger than men. Without her, I would have given up."

"And Richard? When did you last hear from him?"

"Just after the accident. He came to see me in the hospital. He was still at Mount Vernon—the place he was ... at ... and they let him out for a day. He said nothing. He just sat at the end of my bed, staring at me."

"Didn't he write or call? Didn't he make any attempt to see you after he had returned to his mother?"

"No. I think Richard wants to leave all of us. He did say one thing when he visited me in the hospital. I didn't know what to make of it. He said, 'Dad, you know how I have always wanted to be there. Well, I *am* there.' Richard was always given to cryptic pronouncements, so I just nodded and said, 'That's good, son,' or something equally banal. What could he have meant?"

I told him everything I have told you—about Richard's fits, the visions he had in them, his dreams, the notebooks. Richard's father listened silently, his head on one side.

"I'm so ashamed," he said finally. "Why could he never tell me? Why could he never trust me enough? I used to mock his mother for her religion. Richard's mother can be very long-suffering, you know. She had a particular 'I forgive you everything' look that drove me crazy. And

163

I wanted Richard to be robust, American. What a fool I was. Who is this Mother, do you think, that he talks about in the notebooks? Have you met her?"

"I have no idea who she is, or really what Richard is writing about, but I respect it. He writes as if he *knows*."

"How can anyone *know*?" Richard's father was suddenly testy, almost growling. He relaxed. "You see how the whole subject riles me. Of course, I might be jealous of Richard's experiences. We can be jealous of anything, can't we? Some people are even jealous of my paralyzed leg. Because of Mary's devotion, I think. Can you imagine being jealous of a man with a paralyzed leg because he is *loved*?" He laughed loudly. "But I would try hard not to be jealous of Richard."

"I think you would manage it."

"I would try. When he was a child we were so close. He would tell me everything, bring me his spiders—"

"*Spiders?*"

"You didn't know of Richard's love for spiders? First it was snakes and then spiders. We used to feed them together. Spiders need a lot of water, you know. You feed them with a syringe. The first drawings he ever did were of webs. You see that door over there—the second white one on the left from the kitchen? That's Richard's room. Used to be. Go in and take a look."

I walked over and opened the door. The room was empty except for a small bed and a bookshelf. Then I saw them. Above the bed, stuck to the wall. Several drawings of webs. They were clearly done by a child—the lines were wavery—but what was startling was that each web was different, and differently colored. There were blue webs, purple webs, one red one with a face in it, smiling.

164

And in the center there was an orange web with a clock in it. A sun of Time rising . . .

I closed the door and turned to Richard's father. I did not know what to say.

He smiled and looked at his watch. "Three twenty-nine. You wait. In a minute—" As he spoke the phone rang. His face lit up. "That is Mary," he said.

"I must leave you."

"Come and see me again. Come with my son."

We shook hands, and he shambled off into the bedroom.

And so, Adolphe . . .

I find I understand nothing. I don't mind not understanding, for a change. It is almost a relief. I give up and wait. It is not up to me to make things clear. That kind of clarifying is a joke . . . Things will clear of themselves, if they do.

Don't die yet, Adolphe. We have a long way to go together.

I am haunted by Richard's orange web with the clock in it. Remember the clock in the Georges Cain, with the hands frozen at midnight? Richard's clock is set at one. A new time?

The words that Abdul said to me come back again and again: "Remember the man you met in the city of mosques." They seem very important, but I can make nothing of them. Which city, for god's sake? On the last count I've been in about thirty "cities of mosques."

Patience. I can't wait to see Anna again.

Carl Huston has left five messages on Antonia's answering machine. Don't worry. I am not answering back.

                                                    Charles

165

Paris

Axolotl—

Do you know, by the way, what an axolotl is? I didn't until Abdul told me yesterday. Apparently they live in caves in Mexico and stay in a retarded state until they are transplanted elsewhere, when they become salamanders and god knows what else. I'm probably getting it all wrong. Anyway, they can transform themselves almost miraculously given a little light.

Well, you are doing well in the light. There are bags of it about at the moment. A salamander would be a good thing for you to become, considering the fire you seem to pull.

Loved the father. Can it be that men are changing? Too late for me, of course. But I had my fun. So what if I got beaten up, called filthy names, etc., etc.? I rose above it. I swished my skirts and went on to become the radiant monster I am. Crucifixion doesn't suit everyone, though.

As for that sentence "Don't die yet," pixie, let me warn you. I have no intention of dying for a while.

I'm not in the slightest surprised about Richard and the spiders. This whole business will get a lot madder before the end.

I asked Abdul about the man and the mosque. He got very cryptic and lofty. I can't stand him when he's in that sort of mood, so left it at that. He did vouchsafe one piece of info, however. He said, "It's not long now." *What's* not long now? If I knew as much as Abdul does I'd just *say* it. But that's me. Say it, broadcast it. I'd buy my own television station and appear on it every night. "Adolphe calling, Adolphe to World, Adolphe to World

. . ." But Abdul likes to lurk in labyrinths and keep mum. Thinks it gives him dignity. If he'd been a queen and been beaten up a few times . . .

I saw the doctor yesterday, by the way. He says I'm a miracle. He says he doesn't know how all my organs are still functioning, but they are, after a fashion. Then he said, "You are the most cheerful terminal patient I have ever had." "Doctor darling," I said, "*what* a compliment!" He smiled happily. Really, he is a most idiotic man, and if he didn't look like Omar Sharif I think I'd go off and die on my own and stop keeping him in platinum cuff-links. But if one has to die, better see something hand-some on one's deathbed. My mother used to say that. After a lifetime of repression, she suddenly became *abandoned* in her final leukemia. How sad that it takes the slow death of all one's cells to make one human.

Two days ago the Tibetan turned up again. You re-member—when I woke up from the visions he had gone. And he went out of my life for weeks. I wasn't worried. I felt we should see each other again. Abdul's been keeping me occupied with dolphins, humming-birds, termites, axolotls and all the rest. Transforming creature by creature into what seems like the entire an-imal kingdom does take up one's time.

The Tibetan rang me up from the place Colette and told me to get there immediately.

I groaned. "I'm sick. I haven't left my room—"

But he had hung up.

So, did I go? What do you think? I wrapped myself in my mink, slapped on some makeup, swallowed a fistful of pills, listened to Callas singing "Un bel di," and tot-tered down to a taxi. I totter wonderfully these days. I met Odile de Valois on the stairs.

"Adolphe darling, I haven't seen you for ages. We *must*

get together soon. A *dîner intime*. Just the two of us."

"Just the two of us and a tape recorder. I know your *dîners intimes*."

She laughed. She is shameless and loves to show off her excellent false teeth. "A tape recorder. What an amusing idea!"

Everyone in Paris knows Odile tapes her friends' phone and dinner conversations.

"I'll miss you, you know, Adolphe."

"Don't bury me yet. I'm not one of your husbands. I don't die to order." (I didn't actually *say* that, pixie, but I thought it.)

I also thought, thank god for the Odiles of this world. One would be tempted to think there was something in Society if it wasn't crawling with them.

I stopped tottering while she was looking. It would have given her too much pleasure. The monsters keep us on our toes.

On to the place Colette, where—in the clear winter sunshine—reading *Le Monde* at the central table (a bit showy, don't you think?) and wearing the most hideous orange bow tie, sat my Tibetan. He gave me a dazzling smile.

"What a tie," I said, sitting down.

"You don't like it."

"I'm jealous."

"Don't be jealous." He was genuinely alarmed. "Jealousy is a very harmful emotion. I'll give it to you." He was about to take it off. I stopped him just in time.

"My jealousy's passed now."

"That is the way with bad emotions. Watch them. Let them pass." He stood up. "We must go."

"I've only just—"

But he was striding off into the Palais Royal. I followed him briskly. Odile and the Tibetan have this in common, they both stop me tottering. Oh, the Palais Royal on a winter morning with frost still on the leaves and white light dancing in the fountains! I tried to stop and take it in. The Tibetan turned to me.

"You love this place, don't you?"

"I lost my virginity here at sixteen."

"You lost it at seventeen, in Nice." It is no good trying to shock one's masters. "In Nice," he repeated, a little vulgarly, I thought. "To a Comte de Charenton."

"You win," I said.

He smiled and shrugged his shoulders.

"Where are we going?"

"You'll see."

We were passing under the windows of Colette. I waved to her ghost . . . The Tibetan led me out into the streets behind the Palais Royal. They were full of young Americans looking bored and knocking into one with their backpacks. We came at last to the entrance of a small alley I had never been in, the galerie Vivienne. "Close your eyes," the Tibetan said. He steered me forward about fifty yards. "You can open them now," he said with a giggle.

There above me was a dirty glass dome. A web. I smiled weakly.

"We must be allowed our little games," said the Tibetan. "There's a café fifteen yards away. We'll sit there."

I was feeling rather faint by now; the pills and Maria were wearing off. The Tibetan started rubbing my back vigorously. "Don't worry," he kept saying. "You are strong."

"Am I strong *enough*?"

169

"Poor Adolphe," he said softly, "I wish all this could have come earlier, when you were well. But that couldn't be."

"There are some things even you can't arrange?"

"Exactly!"

Twenty yards later we came to a café. The inside is painted gold (I'm *not* joking) and its name is *too* wonderful. The A Priori. Go and see for yourself. And there was Abdul sitting beaming in a corner, a ziggurat of ham sandwiches in front of him. I dislike it when he beams. No one should beam with teeth like his. I think the last dentist he saw was in prewar Alexandria.

"My dear Abdul. No more animal books for me today. I don't think I could cope."

"Just a teensy-weensy article on the orb-web spider and a quotation from Henry James."

"No, Abdul. No, no."

He stopped beaming and started sulking. Abdul sulks like Osmin in Mozart's *Seraglio*—loudly, and in purple.

"Don't you want to hear about the orb-web spider building webs in gravityless conditions?" said Abdul.

"It seems to me perfectly obvious it could. I've been doing so myself for as long as I can remember."

It was not a very good joke, but Abdul laughed. He is infuriating but loyal.

"You are looking very well today, Abdul."

"My doctor says I shouldn't be alive. I'm a miracle!" he stood up before I could stop him and spun round on his heels. "I'm a miracle!" he repeated, eyeing the Vietnamese waitress in the corner, who giggled.

"The heady days of King Farouk are over," I said. "Fat men should not dance in cafés."

"Fat men," beamed Abdul, "are the kings of life. Fat men are the Rameses III of existence."

"I agree," said the Tibetan annoyingly. "My master in Tibet was very fat. We used to say, 'Never leave a bag of sweets near the master or they will be all gone.' After Enlightenment, you know, it must be very difficult to go on without little rewards."

"It must be," I said.

"It is," Abdul drawled.

"Yes, it is," Blue-Eyes said, taking a large ham sandwich and eating it like Charles Laughton eats chicken legs in *Henry VIII*. He didn't quite throw it over his shoulder, but he might have done.

"Now, why have you brought us here?" I asked.

"Oh, my dear friend," Blue-Eyes smiled. "Always impatient. Isn't it enough for us to be together, the three of us?"

"Don't be sly with me," I said. (I revere Blue-Eyes, but sometimes . . . I don't think I'm made to be a disciple, exactly.)

Blue-Eyes finished chomping and looked from Abdul to me. He took both our hands between his and rubbed them. "You are jolly nice men," he said. I swear he said "jolly nice."

"Abdul is a lot nicer than I am," I said.

"This is true," Abdul drawled again, picking one of the blackest of his teeth. "Even my grandmother who found fault with Allah himself used to say, 'Abdul, you are as sweet as the song of the bulbul in spring, as refreshing as the brook of Khezr.'"

"Liar."

Blue-Eyes coughed. "My dear friends," he began, "I have brought you here to tell you a little about myself, my long search for truth, and its conclusions. Not that the search for truth can have conclusions, only directions."

"Well said," said Abdul, bringing out his little gold notebook and writing in his laborious childish hand "No Conclusions Only Directions."

"If you're going to write down everything he says," I said, "we'll be here all night."

"All this Western *hurry,* Adolphe. Master and I understand each other. We are Orientals. We have time."

The Tibetan coughed. "Actually, we have two hours at the most. Then the time stops being propitious and I have to leave."

"So much for *you,* Abdul."

Abdul stuck out his thick white tongue.

Blue-Eyes said, "You two are worse than the youngest monks in my monastery at home. We used to be very severe with them."

"Be very severe with Adolphe," Abdul said. "He takes to punishment better than I do. I just become sullen and eat sweets."

"Abdul—"

"Don't threaten me, Adolphe. Your eyes go all googly. It doesn't suit you."

"My dear friends, I must ask you to be quiet." Blue-Eyes used a tone no one could argue with. So that is what you learn lying on rocks in the snow. Silence in the A Priori. I felt my mind clear. He had let us chatter to relax us, then *poof, wham,* down came the hammer of silence . . . I felt very light. The gold walls shone. I thought for a second we were in a Tibetan temple. I noticed that there was no one else in the café but the waitress. How had Blue-Eyes managed that? Ask no questions . . . Blue-Eyes took out of his jacket pocket a box of matches and a small stick of incense. He lit the incense. "May all we say be for the enlightenment of all beings."

"Inshallah," said Abdul.

"Amen," I said.

"The monastery I belonged to," Blue-Eyes began, "was one of the greatest and most ancient in Tibet. It was just outside Lhasa and had the reputation of being among the most austere. That is why I chose it. As a very young man I knew that the one thing I wanted was to pursue the Path of Enlightenment."

Abdul groaned. "As a young man all I wanted to do was to pursue the path of women."

"I made rapid progress and very early went into the three-year retreat that is common to the early stages of meditation. When I came out, the Chinese were taking over my country. My monastery was looted and burned to the ground. Many of the monks were massacred. I went into hiding in the house of some peasants. After a long struggle with myself, I joined the resistance."

"I thought a monk was forbidden to kill," I said.

"I have never and I will never kill anyone. I was not a soldier. I was a spy, a go-between, a translator of Chinese documents. I was caught and imprisoned in one of the camps that the Chinese have up on the edges of my country, in the remote regions of the north. A hard-labor camp where every form of psychological and physical torture was employed. I have been tortured, many times, and seen my friends die.

"When I say I am grateful to the Chinese for what they did to me, do not imagine I am being sentimental. In life you often owe more to your enemies than to your friends. It is your enemies that compel you to marshal your inner forces, their hatred that teaches you the meaning and power of compassion. It is easy to love one's friends—but to love one's enemies, that takes every nerve of spiritual intelligence. Affliction is a supreme teacher if you survive its lessons. I do not want you to think that I learned what I am about to tell you in the ease of a monastic cell; I learnt it in the filth and horror of a camp. I learnt it on the rack."

Abdul looked stricken. The merest mention of physical pain fills him with grief. I have seen him countless times pick up slugs from the paths of the Jardins du Luxembourg and lay them on the grass. It makes walking with Adbul in spring an epic undertaking.

The Tibetan went on. "In the camp I meditated constantly. I was determined never to hate the Chinese. I knew that if they succeeded in making me hate them, then everything I had learnt in the monastery and from my master would be wiped out. I had seen my master die in pain and serenity; I knew it was possible to suffer without rancor, and I was determined to be worthy of him. I meditated on Tara, the goddess of compassion, and said her mantra to myself incessantly, even in my sleep. I prayed to Tara to unmake in me all that was ruthless and afraid, all that made me like my torturers. I prayed to her to *make* me her."

"Om Tare Tutare Sohar," Abdul said softly. "Is that not the sacred mantra of Tara?"

The Tibetan closed his eyes. "Yes. Om Tare Tutare Sohar. I'm remembering a small village high in the mountains of Tibet. It is on a plateau; you have to walk for a day from the nearest town to get there in summer. The plateau is entirely covered with barley. A Tara temple stands there, and it has an old priest whom I often visited. Sometimes we would go and pray in the fields as the sun set. He would say, 'Now we are in the body of the Mother.' The gold of the barley would burn around us, and the scent of the wildflowers hidden in it would bring us joy." He paused. "When they were torturing me I would imagine myself sitting down in that barley and pressing my face into a clump of those flowers."

Abdul groaned, and big tears came to his eyes. It is very annoying how Abdul can materialize tears to order.

"Stop it, Abdul," I said. Isn't that disgraceful? I record it here just in case you think I really have "gone beyond."

Abdul's big tears fell and fell. Abdul is undoubtedly closer to "it" than I am (he's probably praying for me this second).

"Adolphe," said the Tibetan, "clear your heart and listen." He said it very sharply. Again I felt the strong inner silence I had been filled with when he first started to speak.

"Tara used often to come to me," he said abruptly. "She is not distant. If you call her, she comes. When I say she came to me, I do not mean anything but that— something physical, though not necessarily corporeal. I would smell the wildflowers suddenly, at night in my cell; looking out of the cell window, I would see for a moment the central stone square of the prison fill with barley, and the old priest standing in the middle of it, looking at me. Tara would speak to me in the voice of my mother, or of a nun I admired, or sometimes even in my voice as a child. She would speak to me and teach me things. Sometimes I would hear nothing but her laughter—a quiet laughter, like the sound of water bubbling up from an underground spring.

"But it is her teachings I want to tell you about. The experiences are not the essential thing. At first I was only aware of her presence in the ways I have described, sustaining me and giving me courage. Then I became aware that she wanted to tell me something.

"Sometimes she would teach me by premonitions.

One afternoon I heard my mother's voice say, 'Two men are coming into the cell to kill you. Do not resist.' Three minutes later, two Chinese soldiers—part of a group that had for months been trying to get out of me the names of my collaborators—came into the cell. I not only did not resist; I found myself leaving my body and looking at everything that happened as if from a great distance. I watched, for example, the way the corners of the larger soldier's mouth twisted; I remember noticing the strength of his forearms as he lifted his right arm to hit me, and thinking, 'He must come from peasant stock. Only a farmer's son who worked all his youth in the fields could have arms like that.' I felt no rancor, no fear. Then a strange thing happened. The men left the room as suddenly as they had entered it. They did not touch me. The man who had raised his arm lowered it. There was a sort of panic in the way they left the room.

"For violence to explode there has to be an answering vibration of fear or anger or hatred in the victim. She was teaching me that if there was no such vibration, violence *could not happen.*

"It was as if I had become her for those moments. I remember feeling very uncomfortable, re-entering my body. Singed, almost. As if the presence that had inhabited it was made of some kind of fire.

"Tara used to appear to me in dreams. Once she took me to a temple somewhere in India. It was by the sea. This time she was the nun I admired, but dressed in a sari. She said 'Look,' pointing to a sculpture of Parvati. 'That is me, under another name.' And I understood that Tara is just one of the names of the Mother. One of Her hundred thousand names.

"She took me into the temple itself and there she

changed. At first her face became sweet, like the face of a dancer. Her whole body altered. Then it became terrible, and I could hardly bear to look at it. She shouted, 'Look at me. Do not turn away.' And as I looked at her face I saw buildings burning, an army of rats crawling over corpses, ditches full of the dying. I kept gazing at this terrible face and it changed again. It became calm and wide as the sky, and in it—or rather, reflected on it as if on a screen—I saw a long quiet white street by the sea. There was a golden light along the street and figures walking down it. Only they were not walking, they were gliding. They did not seem to be talking, but they were obviously communicating with each other, because on their faces—which were like our faces, only more beautiful and supple—there were expressions of great happiness.

"'This is what I am preparing,' the voice of myself as a child said. 'This is the future. This is the future, here, on earth. Not elsewhere.' And here my child-voice began to laugh. 'The Divine Life will be here, in these streets.' This was the first of the dreams in which I felt her telling me of a new plan for mankind, a new revelation unlike those to be found in any religion, even the profound one in which I had been trained.

"The daily beatings continued, the starvations, the snow falling on the stone courtyard outside." Blue-Eyes rubbed his hands. "I am going to tell you her greatest and most humorous revelation, my friends."

"I can hardly wait," said Abdul, and again I felt like kicking him. Only Abdul, of anyone I have ever met, can get away with the *totally* ingenuous.

"Yes," Blue-Eyes repeated, his eyes widening, "what she told me is indeed marvelous."

He really did say "indeed marvelous," which proves that under the impact of emotion even the grandest of us can talk like an English curate.

"The first time it happened, it happened on the toilet," Blue-Eyes said. Abdul and I glanced at each other a little nervously.

"I was sitting on the tin basin each prisoner was given to do his business in. I heard my mother's voice. 'This is what *they* will see.' I understood by 'they' the figures of the future I had seen in that white street. Then the experience started. Every substance in the cell started to change, slightly, very slightly. The stone floor shone, not from a light from without but as if each atom of the stone were revealing its secret light. The dirty towel on the wall began to shine. That, however, is almost normal. What was absolutely new was what was happening to my body."

Abdul leaned forward eagerly. One has only to mention the word *body* for Abdul to become excited. "Yes?" he whispered. "Yes?"

"I can only say," said the Tibetan after a long pause, "that my body was spreading itself over the whole world."

"You were sitting on a toilet—a tin toilet—in a camp in North Tibet and your body was spreading itself over the whole world."

Blue-Eyes looked at me. "Of course it sounds absurd. But that is what happened." He shrugged his shoulders. "I shall go on."

"Yes!" said Abdul. "Yes!"

Suddenly I thought, I have a choice. Either I go out of the A Priori now and forever, leave these two lunatics to their own devices, or I listen with my whole being and

178

join them, wherever in earth or heaven they are.

It was as simple as that, I realized. No earthly logic was of any use.

"You will decide to stay," said Blue-Eyes.

"How dare you intercept my thoughts?"

"Please. After all we have been to each other . . ." The Tibetan went on. "My body spread over the whole world. It had ceased to be solid. It had become a series of pulsing waves. I realized that everything is nothing but these waves and they all beat to the same vibration. I looked about me and saw everything both moving at an extraordinary speed and staying completely still at the same time, and in a calm light. I realized that all that our physical senses receive as reality is nonsense. I realized too, as I was having the experience, that there was *nothing mystical* about it, *nothing otherworldly.* This consciousness was of this world, and open to everyone. It was nothing to do with leaving the world, with that liberation, that moksha or nirvana many Eastern thinkers write of—it was to do with *completely entering matter,* becoming the *real* matter, the true matter that we, all things, potentially are. Something that had always troubled me about the Buddhism I had been reared in made itself clear. I did not, I realized, want to *leave* this world; I did not want that which I understood by nirvana. I wanted this—to be here, to be *absolutely* here, in this spreading through matter, in this timeless, deathless experience of matter.

"I did not look at things; I *was* things. I did not look at the dirty towel; I *was* it, and it shone and rejoiced with me. Into this matter, this transfigured matter, no death can enter. Or rather, death and life are two sides of the same golden vibration and one enters and re-enters one and the other a thousand thousand times a second."

The Vietnamese waitress came and stood sulkily by the table.

"Anything else?"

Abdul and Blue-Eyes were both in trances, so I had to summon my remaining marbles and say "Three orange juices."

We all three repeated "Three orange juices" very solemnly, as if it were a mantra. The girl thought we were mocking her and slouched off, muttering *Vieux cons.*

"The second experience was when I was being tortured—"

"Abdul, if you start to cry . . ."

"Stop it, you two. I want your complete attention."

The waitress brought the orange juices.

"I was being tortured," the Tibetan said matter-of-factly, "not especially badly. The routine cigarette stuff. But I had been starved for a week and so felt particularly sensitive."

Abdul's eyes filled with tears. I was good; I looked away and said nothing.

"In fact, I fainted," Blue-Eyes went on. "It was as if I had fallen into a vast black slimy hole. Have you ever been in the catacombs of Paris?"

"No," I said.

"It was as if I had fallen into a catacomb. I came to a very small hole in the wall, far smaller than my body. I knew I had to get through it, and that nothing less than the Mother's help could make it possible. No sooner had I asked for her than I was through the hole, in the other room. I heard a voice say, 'This is the first and last room. This is Room A and Room Z in your language.'

"It was then that I realized where I was. As a young monk I had always been curious about Western science. The Dalai Lama himself has a great respect for Western science, and many of the high lamas are experts at one or another branch. I was most interested in biology, and had managed at great expense to get a modern textbook from India through a Nepalese trader. I was, my dear friends, inside a cell. Inside an original cell of the body. I had entered the heart of a cell of matter. A light began around me. A light like the one I had seen on the toilet—one that shone from within rather than from without. Not a bright light, a soft gold-gray light that permeated everything. I had again the physical sensation of being spread out. And then I heard it. The humming I mentioned before. Only this time it was coming from all around and within me. Thousands and thousands of different tiny voices." His face lit up. "And all these voices were saying the mantra of Tara, the sacred mantra of the goddess of compassion."

Abdul clapped his hands. I had no idea what to make of anything.

"Don't you understand?" said the Tibetan. "Must I spell out everything?"

Abdul had closed his eyes and seemed completely gone, so it was left to me to say, "What you have said is beautiful, poetic, and totally incomprehensible. Spell it out."

The Tibetan looked at his watch. "What a relief," he said. "We have twenty minutes left."

"Enough to explain the future of mankind?"

"Oh, yes." He smiled, meeting my irony full on. "Oh yes, indeed."

Abdul made a sort of soft whinnying sound which I

suppose he thought of as ecstatic. It probably *was* ecstatic, come to think of it. Abdul had *seen*. I was still in the dark.

"Look, Adolphe. It is simple, so very, so completely simple."

"Too simple, perhaps."

"Don't be frightened." The Tibetan's voice was soft.

"Anything else?" The Vietnamese waitress again.

"Nothing else," Abdul murmured from his trance. "Nothing else."

"Abdul, I'm warning you . . ."

Abdul smiled and sighed, a soft plump angelic sigh.

The Tibetan went on. "When I came to from fainting, I was still on the table being tortured, but my body went on in the state of bliss it had been in my dream. And I could feel all its cells, all its hundred trillion cells, saying in tiny voices, 'Om Tare Tutare Sohar,' again and again in an unending blissful chorus. The point is, you see, Adolphe, that the cells of the body can be altered."

"Altered?"

"Up to now, through all their millions of years of development, they have been taught only the lessons of death, illness, resistance, strife, war. And they have obeyed those lessons to the end. Cells have an imbecilic good will."

"I shall take your word for it."

"Not for much longer." He looked at me strangely and went on. "This good will is our good fortune. What I learnt in that descent into matter on the rack is that this message that the physical apparatus—the 'mental physical'—sends to the cells, a message made up of millennia of fear and struggle, is not an eternal message at all, but a temporal one that can be altered. And that the power of the Mother can alter it by her mantra. A mantra is a sacred sound that reorganizes reality. The cells can be made to say the mantra of eternal life. Their endless monotonous repetition of 'death, death' can be changed to the mantra of life. This is not fantasy; not mysticism; not even miraculous. The miraculous is only the natural that we do not yet understand. When the cells are changed in this way, the body will be transformed, will become the body I saw in that vision and you (if I am not mistaken) saw in your flat—supple, golden, immortal."

"This is madness."

"No, my dear friend. This is simplicity. This is normality. It is as ordinary as that sign over there. Look at it."

I looked across the street. It was the sign of a travel agency, Chemins du Soleil. Across from the A Priori, the Ways of the Sun.

"One day scientists will understand all this too. They are already beginning to suspect that consciousness affects matter. Well, they have a lot of surprises in store! In the end science and mysticism will link hands and do the sublime tango of the future."

"If we have time."

"We will have time. There will be catastrophes, but the race will not perish." Blue-Eyes chortled at my discomfiture.

"You are certain. How can you be? You yourself said it was Kali-Yuga . . ."

He smiled. It was obvious that whatever knowledge he had could not be communicated in any words that I could understand. He patted my hand as if to say, "Have faith, be at peace."

"Will I dance the sublime whatsit of the future? In this old body?"

He did not answer me. He said, "You can open your eyes. Who knows what you may yet see?"

Abdul opened his eyes at that very moment, anxious as ever not to miss anything.

"I shall go now," said Blue-Eyes. "Om Tare Tutare Sohar."

I repeated the mantra falteringly, feeling helpless and ridiculous but also elated.

Blue-Eyes paused at the door. "One more thing. The Mother is on earth. To give birth to the future. You will know where She is before you die," he said, turning to me, "and so will you, Abdul. I have prayed for this and it will be granted."

Abdul's eyes widened. The Tibetan waved once, solemnly, and then said, "When you are leaving, look up at the glass web."

We did. In great gold letters circling the web is *Expansion Biologique Française*.

I have tried to be faithful to all the abruptness, hilarity, lunacy, of all this. I have tried to be honest about all my misgivings, my jealousy . . .

What can it all mean? I go over it all in my mind, again and again. I cannot deny my vision. I cannot deny Blue-Eyes's power.

I am at a loss. I realize I cannot understand it with my conscious mind. God knows, I have very little conscious mind left, and never did have much. But can one send it away altogether and so achieve nakedness?

I'm going to have a bash. Why not? I have nothing left to lose. My hair's gone. Why not my false reason?

She is on earth, is She? I'm ready for Her. I must say

I enjoy the idea of "it" being on earth. I always found the idea of heaven or whatever almost as boring as hell. All those angels with lutes, ugh! My Egyptian aunt used to say, "Going to heaven would be a fate worse than death." Even the Mohammedans with their houris didn't get it quite right, did they?

The Divine Life on earth. A much better idea. Here-andnow, nowandhere. I must stop this celestial drivel and have a bath.

Celesto-gran

P.S. I'm starting to talk out loud to Her. After all, if She's on earth, She can hear me. I say things like, "Show your hand, Ma." The direct approach. I have a feeling She would prefer that to false reverence. What do you think She's wearing?

P.P.S. Not Opium, I hope.

Final P.S. I hope you noticed the three orange juices in the above. Even pioneers of the new race must keep up their health. Especially pioneers of the new race, come to think of it. There's a lot out there against us, including us (if you know what I mean) (and I fear you do).

·FOUR·

New York

Dear Adolphe—

Yesterday I walked around Central Park in the snow with your letter (when you get letters like *that* you have to go outside and do something). How am I supposed to respond to it? Many passages made me laugh out loud—and not with a very kind laughter, I'm afraid. Goddammit, Adolphe—the café, the Chemins du Soleil, all that Expansion Biologique . . . I know it *happened*. I *know* it happened. But still . . .

Who am I after all to say that things like that cannot happen? Why do I still want to?

Fortunately I have learnt—largely because you have taught me—to listen to my laughter. It did not take a lot of time or wisdom this time to hear my laughter as fear.

What the Tibetan says *is* frightening. No more delicious nirvana; the work has to be done here. Not in the "spirit" or "mind," or even "mystical intelligence"—but in the body. The endlessly disappointing body. It is a lot too much, Adolphe. How are we going to teach all those hundred trillion cells to speak Sanskrit? When we do get the little bastards singing away, won't everything else untransformed in reality go to attack them? Can one transformed body transform the rest of matter? Is transformation really as contagious as all that?

Even the questions seem raving.

So She is here, is She? What the hell does *that* mean?

Then I want to write: well, if She is here, when do we meet Her?

I may be skeptical, Adolphe, but I'm also curious. I am game (I think) for anything. If one is going to make a complete fool of oneself, better do it attempting the absolutely impossible. I suspect that if She is here, she will need the conquistador type around Her, the desperadoes far more than the saints (they can go off to the ashrams and monasteries). She will need those angry and impatient enough with things as they are to think the impossible and to long for it.

And now for Richard. It won't surprise you to find out that your letter made a lot of things clearer in the notebooks. I say "clearer" in the murkiest sense, of course. I took them with the letter into Central Park. Here are some of the things I read with new eyes:

> Materialism is the gospel of death. Death is all it understands. Sometimes I talk to my body and it glows with a confidence beyond transience.

> No good transforming from above. The mistake of psychiatry, all gospels of Consciousness. Who wants more *will?* Who wants to be more *Father?* All notions of the Father bear the imprint of his pathetic divisions, his isolation. Go within. What *is* within? Within the bone, within the flesh. Father is a paranoid with little imagination, and so protects himself with a series of pat formulas about everything. Father has always been teaching

the body the same lesson—fight, fight, struggle, die. But supposing the message changed? Supposing instead of being taught obedience to death, it was taught immortality?

I made a joke up last night which I like. Death is not inevitable—it is just an accident that has always happened. Mother teaches by radical jokes, unlike Father, who is only a farce man. What would it mean to *believe* that joke?

What is clear is that in his so-called madness, Richard has understood a lot of what the Tibetan told you. Madness broke Richard into the new dimensions the Tibetan spoke of. Naturally, his knowledge is not as serene or as methodical as Blue-Eyes's. The Father–Mother stuff is crude. I now think that Richard organized his release from the asylum to set about working with these new forces. What he was doing in the upper reaches of his mother's house was trying to come to terms with what he had experienced, by setting his notebooks in order and—I am certain of this, although there is no direct evidence—by some kind of spiritual practice. God knows *what* kind. I have every fear for him, as beginning spiritual practices without anyone to guide you is one of the most dangerous things anyone can do. And he is not exactly stable, although he is, I believe, in some way at least, partially illumined.

I believe also that he knows I am here and that he in some sense willed it. And that he willed it for my own good and as a gift. How ironic! I imagined that I had been the one to give everything . . . All the tables are turning. And I have found out, too, what Abdul meant about the city of mosques . . .

Yesterday evening after my long afternoon in the park

I decided to visit a friend of mine, James, a writer, who lives on Seventy-fourth Street. He is in his late forties, and one of the few people I trust in New York. Although his apartment is not quite as flamboyant as yours (whose could be!), it is a fantastical and beautiful place. It is full of objects from James's many travels—rugs from Turkey, prayer mats from Morocco, a green vase with dolphins from Chios, even a stuffed hummingbird (you'll be pleased to hear) from Brazil.

During the evening I asked James which was his favorite city. He said, "It changes, every decade. In my twenties it was Paris. In my thirties it was Istanbul. I lived near the Blue Mosque . . ."

I remembered Abdul's words to me about the city of mosques and the blond man and understood them.

It was James saying "I lived in Istanbul near the Blue Mosque" that brought back in detail the two months I spent there, eight years ago. I too lived near the Blue Mosque, in one of the many hotels in that part of Istanbul for which flea-pit is too grandiose a name. The hotel was filthy, but I liked it. It was stacked with layabouts from all over—Swedes resting from working in Indonesia, Americans finding themselves, the usual cosmopolitan riffraff.

There was one man I liked especially, a lanky blond Dutchman who smiled at everyone but never seemed to speak. He had sad eyes with dramatic bags under them, and before I plucked up the courage to ask him about himself, I had seen him sitting in the café below the hotel reading the sermons of Hui-Neng.

He never seemed to go out. I would leave him in the early morning at his table, and return in the late afternoon to find him still there, a pile of empty coffee cups around him, still reading or writing something in a note-book. One day I saw the cover of the notebook. It was one of the candy-striped, large-margined notebooks you pick up in bazaars in India. So I went over to his table and introduced myself.

"I have been observing you for a while," he said.

"What have you seen?"

"That you never wear matching socks."

At first our speech was formal, but I persisted, and he gradually opened up. He had been born in Jakarta, gone back to Amsterdam to live with his mother's family after both of his parents had been killed in a fire, studied engineering, tried business, hated it, and then, quite by chance, become interested in Eastern philosophy. He had found a book by Janwillem Van de Wetering, *The Empty Mirror,* which told of a stay in a Zen monastery.

"And so I gave up my job and went to Japan," he said matter-of-factly, "and I stayed for four years."

"Four years in a Zen monastery?" I was impressed.

He looked at me amusedly. "It is not so hard. Even meditation can become a habit. That was the trouble. I found Zen too dry. As a child in Jakarta, I had seen the famous Indonesian puppet shows. They are very rich, and I went often with my father's chauffeur, who would explain the myths to me. In the monastery in Japan these myths came back to me, and I decided to go to India and see what Hinduism was like."

I looked blank.

"The myths were Hindu ones. From the Mahabarata and the Ramayana. I decided it would be better to re-turn to the source, to India, than to my childhood."

"So you went." I had realized by now that he was a man of decision.

"Of course."

I told him of my childhood in India, of my love of Indian things and philosophy (the little I knew of it then). He listened attentively, as if he were weighing me, and said, "I think I can tell you then why I am here." He paused. "I am waiting."

"Waiting?"

"I am waiting for a friend I met in India."

"Does he know you are here?"

"You had better know the whole story." He looked away over my head at the open door. "Very soon after I arrived in India I met an English boy. I met him at Sanchi, by the great stupa there. He was camping out on the hill nearby, meditating and living simply. We became friends. I had spent four years in a Zen monastery, but I had not met anyone there as truthful as he was.

"We pooled our resources and traveled together from ashram to ashram, hoping to find one where we would be able to live. We never did; there always seemed to be something wrong with the atmosphere. In the end, we decided to live alone on a beach in Kerala. In Cannanore, in fact."

I started. Cannanore was a place I had visited as a child. I told him of the long white beach there, curved like a kukri, that I had often visited.

"There are many beaches like that there. But perhaps it was the same beach. I hope it was, because then we should have shared one of the best places on earth." He fell silent. Then he said, "He and I were happier living on that beach than I could describe. My friend and I lived for each other and the God we felt always around us."

He looked at me to see if I was skeptical of what he

was saying. He saw that he had moved me, and went on. "But then I realized that I had to leave. My friend is much younger than I. I am thirty-six, and he is only just twenty-two. He has his life before him. We could not stay on that beach, however perfect our life was there. So I just left without telling him. One night when he was sleeping, I took the morning train to Trivandrum and from there flew to Bombay. From Bombay I came here. I had never been to Turkey and thought it would be a good place to piece myself together in."

"Didn't you regret leaving him like that?"

"Regret is too weak a word."

"You said you are waiting for him? Why?"

"Because there are things I think he is ready to understand. And I must explain them to him."

"Does he *know* you are waiting for him?"

"No, he does not. Nor does he know where I am. But he will come. He will come soon."

For a moment, Adolphe, I thought he had gone mad.

He smiled. "I see you don't believe what I have just said. I do not blame you. I would not have believed it before I traveled in India and loved him. There are some things only life can reveal to you, and only then if you are receptive."

I was annoyed at his sibylline tone. "Like what?"

"Like the power of patience. The power of patience when it is linked to love."

"So you mean to tell me that you are sitting in this sleazy café in Istanbul willing a boy who might be anywhere to come and meet you because you have unfinished business and you want to say you love him?"

"Yes. That is it exactly. But you have missed out one thing from your little summary."

195

"What is that?" said I.

"The power of God."

He stood up. It was a wonderful line to stand up on, worthy of you, in fact.

I said, "I really did not mean to offend you. Please sit down. There are many things I do not understand. What you have said seems unlikely but not impossible. I'm sorry if I appeared smart."

He sat down. "Do you play poker?" he asked, drawing a greasy pack of cards out of his jacket pocket. We played most of the night, and I lost every game.

Three days later, while we were eating together in the Pudding Shop, just down the road (only you, Adolphe, will believe this. I swear it as I am an Englishman and the descendant of a race of military men with moustaches), *the boy walked in.*

I was sitting with my back to the door, talking. The Dutchman as usual kept his eyes on the door. Then his face lit up. I write "lit up," but that is far too ordinary a description of what happened. His face *blazed.* I turned round. Walking towards us was one of the most beautiful boys I have ever seen, in blue jeans and jacket, his white shirt open to the waist. He was walking straight towards the Dutchman. The boy sat down next to me. The Dutchman and he gazed at each other. "How did you get here?" the Dutchman asked.

"I was flying from Israel to Cyprus. The plane got diverted. I'm only in Istanbul for tonight."

In all of Istanbul he had chosen on his one night there this place, of all . . . I was astonished, but at the same time calm. When it happened—the very thing I had three days before thought absolutely unlikely—I was not surprised. I was exalted, but not surprised. Isn't that odd?

I got up, shook hands with them both, and said, "You have many things to talk about. I must be going."

Now do you understand, Adolphe, why I have told you this story at length? Richard is waiting for me as that man waited in Istanbul for his friend. I *know* it. That is what Abdul meant by "remember the man in the city of mosques." He wanted me to remember the example I had already seen of the power of love and patience. I think I know where Richard is waiting. Not exactly. But the general location. He is waiting for me in the town where we first met, in Rhodes, upstate New York.

I will take the bus tonight.

Will you please tell Abdul to be a little more explicit in future? But perhaps even the Abduls of this world can't be, or shouldn't be. Or something.

But anyway, I'm going. And by Greyhound. Greyhounds are always so full of crazy people, I'll just be one more of the shakers and mutterers. Write to me at the post office in Rhodes.

Charles

Before I recount what happened in Rhodes, I must put here the letter I received from Anna three days later at the Rhodes post office. Adolphe had sent it on by express post.

ANNA TO CHARLES AND ADOLPHE

Mahabalipuram

Thank you for the big bundle of letters, which arrived in Bangalore looking like a squashed turtle. I hope you two don't mind it when I say that I understood every word of them. I know you think I'm slower than you in the "metaphysicals," but I have news for you, you two male spiritual snobs. It all seemed kosher to me. But then, I am in India, where no dream could be as fantastical as the reality I see every day in a side street or out of the cracked window of a bus, and where the light is exactly that light you describe as belonging to the new world—golden, lucid, and soft as a ripe mango.

So much has happened since I last wrote.

I left Benares ten days ago. On the last day, I went to a fortuneteller. Actually, he called me in. I was wandering in a sort of trance down one of the small cowpat-caked alleys round my hotel when I heard this voice, very deep, speaking in a most cultured, ripe English: "Madam, would you care to step into my little shop? I have things to tell you." I turned round and saw this *tiny* man. When I say tiny I mean about four foot six at the most, very old, with an improbably large head. Not at all ugly; beautiful in fact, with combed and parted white hair and a face as wrinkled as a walnut.

I went in. The whole place was scented with incense— he had placed large sticks of the stuff at each corner. A small boy lay on a mat, sleeping.

We sat on a gold-circled carpet covered with bread-crumbs. It was late afternoon, and the astrologer opened three or four windows in the front, and the late quiet sun covered us.

Suddenly he hopped up. "Of course," he said. "How happy."

I stared at him.

"Now at last I shall know where Ramsgate is."

There I was, sitting cross-legged, expecting Wisdom,

and this tiny big-headed sage was asking me where Ramsgate was.

There was no time to flee or question him because he flitted about the room, pulled a book from under some cushions, fell to the floor, and opened it at my feet. It was an ancient insect-riddled map of Great Britain with all sorts of shaky circles inked all over it.

"You want to know where Ramsgate is," I said in my most convent voice. "Why didn't you look in the index?"

"My dear madam, the eyesight is very failing. Too much reading, reading."

I peered at his eyes. They were sore and sunken, like an alcoholic's the morning after. I pointed out Ramsgate. "Now I have shown you where Ramsgate is, could you tell me why you wanted to know?"

"Oh, madam." He sighed, as if the telling would reveal wonders too great for anyone's understanding. "How to begin?"

I thought, listen to the horns and the sadhus singing in the street, listen hard, otherwise you will think yourself in some absurd dream. Watch the crease in his white baggy trousers.

"Two weeks ago I was sitting on my steps, madam, and this very fat man came by. English sahib, madam. I am very old but he was very very old. With moustache. Very big trousers because very big bottom. I am liking this man. So I called him, 'Sahib, please do me the honor to enter,' and he made a funny noise between his teeth and came in. 'You an astrologer.' 'I most famous astrologer of Benares.' 'Well, I am a Catholic.' 'I am liking Catholics, Protestants, everything. Every man is holy. Every path leads to God.' 'Do you really think so?' Funny noise again. 'This is my religion, dear sir. All paths lead to him.' 'Good man,' he says, 'good man.' We have tea. Then he says, 'Have you heard of Lourdes?' 'Once,' I said, 'I had a French lady in here. She had been cured in Lourdes.' 'Yes, yes,' he said, 'we need an English Lourdes.' 'An English Lourdes?' 'Yes. To revive the faith. We need the Virgin Mary to appear in England, some- where close to London, so everyone could visit the place easily.' 'But, honored sir,' I said, 'the Virgin will appear where she is believed in. She will not appear just any- where.'

"At this he got very angry. 'England just anywhere? *Just anywhere?* She appears in Frogland, she appears to those bloody bog Irish.' What is this Frogland and bog Irish? 'Why will she not appear in England?' I said noth- ing, and I am drinking my tea calmly. Perhaps this man is mad. But I am liking his trousers and his moustache. I make joke. 'Why, dear sir, don't you make her appear?' His face lit up. 'Oh, I knew you would understand. You have read my very thoughts. I have chosen the place for her appearance. *Ramsgate.* It should be *Ramsgate.* That is in Kent and it is near London and it is *respectable.* No blacks—forgive me—and no Irish. I shall hire three local children and a pretty girl.'

"'Most honored sir, are you telling me that you are planning to *fake* the appearance of the Virgin? Is this not risky?' 'Everything is a risk in life.' 'So what can I do for you?' 'You can tell me if Ramsgate is a holy place.'

"I thought for a moment. If I tell this man that Rams- gate is holy, then he will do this crazy thing. So I closed my eyes, I whispered a song to Kali under my breath, and I pretended to look in some books. Then I said, 'Ramsgate is *very* bad place, dear sir. Very bad for Virgin, for everything. I see—oh god—I see prison for you, a big black car, and your wife, I see her with tears the size of peacock's eggs. Dear sir, do not do this thing.' 'Are you certain?' 'You are asking me this thing? The adviser to maharajahs, holy men, Indira Gandhi herself? If you go on with this thing to make the Virgin appear at Rams-gate, there will be death and destruction.' His face, dear madam, went as pale as the top of his cane. I was sorry for him. I said, 'Why do you not pray very hard to the Virgin? Ask her to come to London. I have read about London. Ask her to appear in Piccadilly Circus. This very central place. Very holy.' He looked happier. 'Very good idea, old chap,' and he gave me a hundred rupees. I only asked for eighty but he was so happy. 'Piccadilly Circus. Right in the middle. In the middle of the after-noon . . .'"

The astrologer hugged his knees and let out a long whinnying laugh. Then he said, looking at me, "To the eyes of love, my dear madam, Mother is everywhere. Why ask her to be anywhere? She will come where she wants. She will appear where she wishes. It is her game. We cannot direct it."

"I rather like the old boy for wanting to."

"Oh no, dear madam. People like him are dangerous. They believe, but in bad way. He is thinking his love for the Virgin gives him the right to push her what way he wish. This is bad. She will do what she will do. She is Wisdom; he is small worm."

Then he said, "I am liking you very much. I will tell you everything for free."

I protested. But the old man rattled on. He told me about my mother trying to kill me; he told me how my father made his money; he said that I was bad with money (true enough). Then he said, "You are going south, aren't you?"

"How did you know?"

He smiled. "You will nearly meet someone you think never again to see. You will not stay long in that place."

That surprised me. I had, as you know, planned to return to the ashram for a while—a month or two at least. He rubbed his hands. "My dear madam, let me tell you about your two friends." (He was talking about you.) "You are all lucky, but you must be careful. You are in the greatest web."

"What do you mean?"

He paused a long time. "The web of the Mother," he said finally, scratching his head and looking away.

"You make that sound very frightening. Is she going to eat us?" I was being brisk.

"She eats everyone," he said. "She eats solar systems for tiffin!" He was pleased with that, and repeated it. "Yes, one supernova for tiffin is not unusual. She has cosmic appetite."

I was beginning to find his humor a little wearying.

"You do not have to fear too much," he then said. "You are the one who will find first and help most."

"What do you mean?"

"You will see."

"My dear sir, you are playing with me."

He took my hand in his. "I am glad you are wearing your marriage ring. You were right to bring it." He smiled. "Remember Ramsgate. If you ever go there, think of me." He began to scratch between his toes, and started to sing something. Then he stopped and said, "Music is greatest web. Even the gods are caught in it. The words are from Kabir. I am loving Kabir and he was using Muslim, Christian, all kinds of words. In this song I am singing, God says, 'I am Man's secret and he is mine.'"

His boy sleeping on the mat awoke and rubbed his eyes.

"He has no mother," said the old man, looking at me. "My daughter died two years ago."

"*You* are his mother," I said.

He flashed me a smile. "Oh, madam, you are understanding." Before I could stop him he had laid the boy beside him and touched my feet.

He was not worshiping me, I knew that, not Anna, but something in me or something that I would become. No. It wasn't anything to do with me that he was worshiping; it was the divine in all things. Then he gave me his card: "Sri Bhagwan Gopal, famous astrologer, 103B Lutyens Road. Always open and ready."

That night, my last in Benares, I had my first erotic dream since I came to India. "Anna, really!" I hear you both exclaim. After all that wisdom . . .

How hard it is to speak of the absolutely beautiful without sounding ridiculous. Even with you two I'm shy. I'm writing this sitting cross-legged on the beach at Mahabalipuram, with the sea wind blowing through my (cropped) hair. Every time I put a page down with a stone to keep it from blowing away, my writing gets covered with gold sand. An omen? I accept it. The sea this afternoon is both controlled and abandoned, and the clear strong light on it seems to say, "Go on! Be anything; say whatever you want; I will sustain you; I will inspire you." So here goes.

I said "erotic dream" to titillate you. Actually there is no word for what I dreamt. *Erotic* is too Soho; it's become a word about as really erotic as crumpled tinfoil, or the muscles of those men you see walking with their fixed smiles and model clothes in New York, or the monotonous beat of the music most of my matchless deathless songs are set to.

The dream began with me walking along the same street in Benares as I had been that afternoon. Only instead of ending in a crossroads it ended at the river. The Ganges in my dream was particularly iridescent. It was evening, just in fact the light of the time I had left the astrologer. I arrived at the river. I was wearing, of all things, a black cocktail dress. I think I was even carrying a bag. I felt ridiculous. To come here, to this holy river, wearing *that*. But then I started laughing. God knows, the river has absorbed much more in its time than a woman in a Saint Laurent cocktail dress.

I started to sing "I Get a Kick Out of You." I thought I was safe with Porter—you know it is so *sophisticated*—but no. How could I ever have thought that song "safe"? I found myself invaded by the pathos of my much-lamented sex life. I should put it a little bit more kindly, I suppose, but I don't feel kindly towards myself in those moods. You must know them—the moods when you feel you have never been loved, never been *savored*, etc., etc., etc. I stood there and swayed and lurched like Judy Garland on a bad night.

A small boy appeared, with a turquoise bandana round his head. Remember the boy you told me about, Charles, who rowed you down the river near Mathura? I have met him, in my dream. He had a raft like the one you described, and small silver anklets. I got onto the raft, and it was then I noticed I was wearing sensible shoes! I said, "Can we go to Ramsgate?"

The gate of the ram. You'll see.

The boy nodded, and we set off down the river. I watched his back in the late light. How beautiful those

204

lithe Indian backs are. Every muscle defined and human, made not by machines but by work. His back had
a deep line running through it like a river. I felt very
tender towards the boy; "Anna," I said to myself, "watch
out. It's a sign of senility and desperation when women
go for younger and younger men."

That back in the late light . . . its muscles moving in
rhythm with the ripples in the river.

I looked at the boy again. He wasn't *that* young—
perhaps eighteen. And he seemed as I looked at him to
become stronger, more manly. His hair seemed longer
and more lustrous. He would turn from time to time to
look at me. I could never see his face—it was by then
too dark—but I could see his eyes. They glittered with
amusement.

The raft slipped to the side of the river, to a small
scimitar-shaped beach of white sand. This must be
Ramsgate, I thought, and stepped off. I turned to thank
the boy, but the raft and he had disappeared. I thought,
looking around, should I be frightened? A Western
woman in the middle of nowhere in a cocktail dress . . .
but even as I started to feel the fear I realized it was
rehearsed. I looked around. Reeds, white sand, more
sand, a few bush-covered small hills behind. A slight
wind in the reeds. Nothing to be afraid of.

So I sat down on the sand. I took my dress off and
started to meditate. My mind filled with memories of
sex. At first I resisted them, feeling embarrassed. Then
I allowed them space. I watched them. The memories
were not of sex; they were of the clear and open moments I had known in sex. And mostly, oddly, memories
of my husband. I had forgotten in my rage how much
tenderness there had been between us. Memories of

lying in bed after making love, of sleeping late, of his touching the back of my neck secretly while we were going down an escalator . . . I realized I have made love to many men, but I have only ever known him (that beautiful biblical "known"). That was why I suffered so much when I learnt what I did about him, and why I have looked so frantically since then for someone to give me what he sometimes could. The looking and the disappointment have made me hard, wary—how could they not have done? Sitting on the beach, I felt that hardness dissolve and the memories that I had banished return. They were the truth of our love and the truth of what I needed in love. In meditating on them, centering myself in the remembrance of them, I found that I could recapture their sweetness and strength without the rage that my need had later invented. Although I recognized that the man I was experiencing these things with was "my husband," I freed him in meditation from that label. It was almost as if I was making love to Peter in the past *for the first time,* free of hunger, guilt, rage, possessiveness, that dreadful need "to have and to hold" that has disfigured my life (and yours too, Charles). How strange to make love at last properly with someone you were married to ten years ago, and do it in a dream.

It was then that the music began. "Exactly," I hear you say, Adolphe. "Just as I would do it in a film. Woman on beach, white sand in the moonlight, music . . ."

The astrologer had said, "Music is the greatest web. Even the gods are caught in it." Remember those quarrels we used to have, Charles, about Indian music? You would go into Cecil B. de Mille raptures—"the cosmic shape of it, Anna!"—and I would say, "It is monotonous, I prefer Bach. Gives a girl something to chew on."

Well, I take everything back, I crawl, I eat dust. For the music that night in my dream was Indian. Unlike any I have ever heard—for what sounded like a flute, sitar, and tabla . . . It began with a slow sitar melody. One of those long-breathed aching melodies the Indians love and elaborate with such mastery. I resisted it at first—I was already feeling raw enough and I felt it peeling me further, exposing me to myself more and more, and then I did open. I had to. The music did not seem to be coming from anywhere in particular, but from everything around me—the reeds stirring in the night wind, the sand, the ripples on the dark river. It seemed to be the song of that loneliness, the sound the river and the reeds and sand made together, the sound of their longing for transformation. You told me once, Charles, that an Indian musician playing the beginning of a night raga wants more than anything else to rouse in the listener *vairagya*, longing for the beloved; that music accomplished with its swoops and long plangent calls that feeling of yearning as no other I have heard has ever done. Above me a large red moon was climbing the sky, as if drawn from its hiding place by the music's power. The light it shed on the sand and water was as sad and wide and stark as the sitar's sound. I watched the water in front of me begin to sway. Slowly the ripples on its surface composed loose, almost formal, circles. The music was changing the water. The circles became lines of silver light . . . I was not afraid. I stood up and started to dance. I found my body much suppler than I remembered—a new body, in fact, partially trans-formed, which could be as sinuous as the reeds, as subtle as the ripples on the water. Sometimes I stood still, but felt all my limbs moving *within themselves* as if the dance were going on inwardly. Then the moon seemed to be rising in me and the water's circles expanding through my blood.

A flute entered the music—a breathy, pulsing, North Indian flute. At first it only shaded lightly what the sitar was playing; then, slowly, it began to diverge from the sitar, to dance with it, circling round it. The tabla began too, and the music became steadily more joyful. The light from the moon changed. From its silver, it became a pale but vibrant gold. The sand took all the subtle force of this light and glowed to meet it. The reeds looked like tall pale gold ears of corn. I saw my arms as they moved before me in the dance. They seemed to become the color of the stone at Khajuraho—that light flickering gold. They seemed fuller, riper, now, as if the music had changed my angular European body into an Indian one.

I heard a rustling behind me and turned. The boy who had directed the raft stood there. He was naked and his skin glowed with the pale gold light that had suffused everything. I realized that it was from him that this light had come. He leaned forward and touched a reed. He was looking at me with great gravity, like a mother might look at her sleeping child. I covered my breasts. I felt skinny, old, and absurd. But he came forward and then did exactly what the astrologer had done—he knelt and touched both my feet with his hands. His palms were covered with a scented ointment. He rubbed it on my ankles and my calves. He rubbed it slowly, not looking at me.

Then we made love.

I kept thinking of the phrase from the old Anglican marriage service—the service Peter and I had used:

"With my body I thee worship." I worshiped his body; he worshiped mine.

After we had ended, he took my hand in his and slid off my marriage ring. He put it on his right hand.

I woke in the great fresh calm of an Indian dawn.

The dream has changed me, made me acknowledge old longings and truths I had tried to bury. During these last few years I had begun to despise men for their cowardice, their vanity, their dull and ruthless refusal of passion. God knows, you have heard me enough on all of those topics! I had quite a polished savage routine, didn't I? I was becoming hard out of hopelessness. All this time in India I have been thinking, I will leave my body behind. I will wear my hair cropped. I will lavish my libido on meditation and yoga and reading the Gita by candlelight. A lot of people come out East to escape the clangor of the flesh in the West. But it remains an escape, an evasion. It changes nothing. The dream made me admit I do not want to be a female eunuch, or a shaman with my breasts cut off, or a nun; I want a sexuality transfigured and made divine by love.

Do you remember that statue of the kneeling Tara I took you to see in the Musée Guimet? I have loved it so long without understanding it. Now I see I had idealized Tara, made her too "spiritual," in the narrow Western sense (the sense that has to hack off the spirit from the body). Now I understand that for Tara there is no separation; the turn of her wrists has the wisdom of the Buddhas in it, and the fullness of her breasts is that of a goddess and a lover. All the separate loves dance together in her, shining, and illuminating each other.

The day after the dream, I left Benares and began on my trip down India to Bangalore. I took trains and buses and got off them when I felt like it. I slept in huts by the edge of fields and learnt again the meanings of words like *fire, guest, dawn, hospitality*. The most paradoxical gift of India is to make you fearless to receive the wealth of poverty. It is the wealth of the white empty interior of a hut where you sleep and watch the dawn rise, or the taste of a chapati cooked for you in a field on a bed of smoldering charcoal. It is frightening in the beauty of its purity, because without meaning to, it questions everything by which you have lived, every false desire, every spoiled hope.

The ashram, when I eventually got there, seemed intolerable. When I first came there with Peter, the Baba Ashram was nothing more than a large huddle of waterless huts—we had to go down to the river to get water. That flattered us and made us think we were really living rough; now there is not even that ascesis to boost one's spiritual ego. There are neat little houses with neat little white rooms and neat little beds in each of them, over each of which is a neat little photo of Sri Ramaji, all of them smiling (and one of the good things about old Ramaji was his sudden fits of rage! I've never forgotten him saying to one American girl, "Throw that chewing gum away! How dare you chew gum before the Divine!"). Everything is hygienic, pasteurized, mild, white on white. Even the crows caw *sotto voce*.

Perhaps it is my need to romanticize the past, but surely, I say to myself, it cannot have been like this *then*. Where are the huddles of people discussing the future and reading the Upanishads? Where are the purple shirts and the laughter and the girls from Minnesota singing bhajans off-key and the ex-prostitutes from Montparnasse with their stories of fellating cabinet ministers and white slavery? The late-sixties crowd were spoiled, naive, anything you like, but exuberant at least. The ashram now is a morgue. The East as well as the West has its gray conventions, you know, and the ashram has relapsed into them. I sat next to an old banker from Bangalore who was smugly mocking Gandhi over banana stew: "Poor Gandhi, no sense of the transcendental." I got furious. How dare he patronize Gandhi, who gave up his life for his vision of India, who dared to act in the world. I was very rude. The banker shook his chubby head. I was another action-obsessed Westerner to him, one who did not have a "sense of the transcendental." Damn this version of the transcendental. It has given up the world too easily.

I suppose what I am saying is that fifteen years on I see the ashram business for what it is and always has been—a sort of accepted ritualistic evasion of the world. What were Peter and I doing, after all, but taking a holiday? We had our experiences and took hash under banyan trees and something did shift in us—but what, in the end, did it *mean*? It was not enough to change me much, at any rate. It left a goodish memory, that is all. I couldn't go into the Baba Ashram now. No one I talked to seemed at all thoughtful. There was a listlessness in all the conversations, and a self-righteousness, that were infuriating.

As for Sri Ramaji! Since we came all those years ago he has become world-famous. Blue-rinsed matrons fly in from Florida to drink holy water from his podgy palms; he still materializes for spectators the odd Swiss watch or aquamarine or bank card, and performs the cures for which he became renowned. I believe he has exceptional powers and I respect him for not having traveled like the others, hawking his "divinity," raking in the dollars. Sri Ramaji is not Rajneesh or the Reverend Moon; he has stayed within the dignity of his spiritual tradition. But I think it is an outmoded dignity. I went to several of his darshans and found a tiredness in his eyes and words, a sense of exhaustion. This moved me; I had a sense of how much he had given. But I had no sense that he had any more to give, or that the ideal to which he had donated his life was really a dynamic one. I am using Western words, I know. But I have come to feel that spirituality must not be otherworldly, that we have no time any longer for the whitewashed sanatoria, the flower-gardened mountain retreats. Sri Ramaji is not decadent; but the world he has allowed to grow around him is, just as decadent in its way as Odile's salon or the back rooms of New York. What Sri Ramaji licenses in those who come to him is a renunciation of the world, a smug giving-up.

I have discovered something frightening—I want neither the Western nor the Eastern way of life. So, where the hell does one go from here? I cannot go back to *la vie parisienne;* I cannot run, singing bhajans, into the plump arms of Sri Ramaji. I can no longer go to parties hoping to find The Man; nor can I sit by the river here repressing my sexuality and thinking of the light at the center of the lotus. Both the Western and the Eastern ways of life seem finished, faded, over.

Remember, by the way, the astrologer saying that if I went south I would almost see someone I did not expect to?

On the second day I was there, Sri Ramaji granted my request for an interview. He received me with his usual gentleness, and blessed me and asked after my life.

He asked me if I knew where my husband was.

"No idea," I said. "Married to someone rich, I imagine. Somewhere where he can spend her money fast."

Sri Rama smiled. "Such bitterness is not good for the spirit."

"Such a husband is not good for the spirit."

He laughed and popped a sweet into his mouth. "What would you do if he walked into this room?"

"Throw this banana skin at him."

"I think you are trying to shock me. It will not work. Actually, I think you have been changing towards your husband. Your heart is softer than it has been. This is good."

"Can't we get off the subject of my wretched ex-husband?"

"Then you don't want to know where he is?"

"Do you mean to say you do? Or are you just playing with me?"

He laughed again and popped an even bigger sweet into his mouth. "While it is true I enjoy a joke, I never play with the heart. I know how much you have suffered." He put his hand over his heart. Then he said, "Your husband works at the ashram school ten miles from here. He has been working there for two years. He teaches English and basic medicine and mathematics. He lives in a small room above the school. He is not there now, as he has gone to Madras for a month. You have just missed him." He finished, and looked at me mischievously.

"My dear Sri Ramaji, I know you are a wizard, but I do not believe that even you could change Peter. Peter a schoolteacher in a godforsaken Indian village school?"

"Not godforsaken," Sri Rama said quietly. "Not that. I

did not change him. He looked into himself and found himself. That is all. I change no one. I help them to change themselves. Very few do. That is the sad thing."

I stared at him. "You really are serious, aren't you? Peter is out there, teaching English and mathematics—"

"And basic medicine. Hygiene, mostly." Sri Rama took up a small orange from the bowl at his side.

To my surprise and rage I found my eyes had filled with tears.

"Do not cry," Sri Ramaji said, handing me half the orange. "This is not an occasion for tears. Are you angry that Peter *hasn't* destroyed himself? Are you disappointed that he has found the power to change? Naughty girl. You could go to the village and see the school, and his room. Westerners always want to see things for themselves." Sri Ramaji looked at me as if challenging me to disbelieve everything he'd said. He looked at me, and I looked back at him, holding his gaze and trying to clear my heart.

Someone in the next room had turned the radio on— dreadful Indian film music, very screechy. Sri Ramaji and I smiled at each other.

"I do not think I need to see the school, or his room," I said at last.

Sri Ramaji nodded, but said nothing, as if he were waiting for something else, something further. The screechy film music became two voices, a man's and a woman's, arguing heatedly in fast explosive Tamil.

"I have no right to interfere with Peter now, or to judge him. He is out of my hands. Tell him I send him . . ." I thought of the exact word I wanted. "Tell him I send him hope."

Sri Ramaji put the last slice of orange into his mouth. "He has hope," he said drily. "You hope for yourself. That is more difficult. I will tell him you came and that you wished him well. That will help him a little. It will help you more."

The next four days I stayed mostly in my room, quietly, thinking of what Sri Ramaji had told me, so shockingly. Was that why I had come back, to learn that Peter too could change? I had to learn that to be able to change myself. I had *fixed* Peter in my mind . . . that is the great crime, isn't it, to *fix* anyone? And so stupid. By fixing others we also fix ourselves.

During the four days that followed, I went over every detail I could remember of my marriage with Peter, from our first meetings to the last surreal, sinister, disastrous months. It was not easy: it was in fact dreadfully painful, because I tried to spare myself nothing. At the end I felt able to start to free Peter, not just from my rage, but also from any partial knowledge I might have of him, and so free myself. Rancor remains—how could it not?—the last smoke after a long fire . . . In a while, I believe, it will clear.

What a blessing that clearing will be. It is only now it is beginning to go that I see what darkness I have lived in.

Those days of thought and memory also made me realize I could not, did not want to, stay at the ashram. I respected Peter's decision to do so, but felt distant from it. I had to choose something else, something other . . . Peter might be able to be healed by a return and a making good of earlier intentions; I knew that I could not be. I did not believe in the old "holy" life. I did not know what I wanted. Not that, I was certain. Can you imagine *me* teaching anyone anything? I'd go crazy, or do one of the village children an injury. I am not made to give patient instruction on hygiene, or sit alone in an empty room.

I wrote to Sri Ramaji explaining I could not stay any longer. Just before I was about to leave he came to the door of my room. I was surprised. He hardly ever leaves his quarters. He stood in the doorway.

"You are not angry with me?" I asked.

"Of course not. I came to wish you farewell."

"*Farewell* sounds so final a word."

He smiled sadly. "I shall not be here long now." He took a small brown leaf out of the folds of his dhoti. "Keep this by you. It will protect you."

"What will protect *you?*"

He blinked and laughed. "I shall protect myself. That is the way." He paused. "I am glad you know where Peter is. He will stay until the end."

Something in his tone chilled me.

"What end, Sri Ramaji?"

"Ashrams have an end, like everything else. It is just as well. Everything that is permanent gets very boring."

"Your disciples would be shocked to hear you say that."

"That is their problem." He sat on the bed, swinging his legs. "I am very tired of my disciples," he said. "They all take me seriously. Not like the old days."

"We took you seriously."

"Not *that* seriously. You used to be cheeky. Very cheeky you were. And fierce. Oh my god. I remember thinking, 'One day this Anna is going to kill someone!'"

"But I haven't."

"I am glad you are leaving. For your sake."

216

"Why?"

"Always why? Why? Nowadays no one says 'Why?' Sometimes I feel like saying any bloody damn thing, just to see if *that* would make them say 'Why?'" He stopped swinging his legs and stood up, wheezing slightly.

"Are you all right, swamiji?"

He waved my question away, impatiently, and then said, "You need a woman guru, not a man guru."

I waited.

"For you, all men are children. You are not wrong. You need a woman."

"I'm not sure I need anyone."

He rubbed his hands, ignoring me. "I am not a child, but you are bored with me," he said.

Here I started to say something, but he stopped me. "Never lie," he said. "I respect your boredom. I nearly forgot, I have a little poem for you. Very bad poem. Very short." He drew a crumpled piece of paper out of his robe and straightened it out.

> Come to Her now, in Her silences' tower
> Climb up the steps and ask for Her power
> She has been waiting and has need of you
> Now is your hour to be faithful and true.

"Very bad poem," he said, with relish. "*Worst* poem. Worse than worst poem."

"Who is She?"

He said nothing.

I looked down. "Thank you for the poem."

"Look at you pursing your lips and saying, 'Thank you for the poem.' Very cheeky girl." He turned to go out. I stopped him and touched his feet. "That was not necessary," he said quietly.

I told you I was writing this from Mahabalipuram. The four days I have been here have been exhausting, charged with new thought and feeling. Everything seems to be going at such a rate, I can hardly keep up with myself. And all these transformations happen within the calm that never leaves this place. Is that what makes them seem, if not effortless, then inevitable, as inevitable as the way the sand turns silver and then gold in the dawn? Or have I come to a time when I am no longer afraid of whatever I might think, and so can change without too much self-consciousness? Whatever the explanation, I have to restrain myself from dancing on the sand. It would amuse the old boys who come out on the sand to do their yoga. No doubt they've seen it before.

Of all the sculptures here there is one I have come not merely to love but to need. I visit it every morning and every evening. You will remember it, Charles: the one of the goddess Durga striking down the Asura.

The goddess is surging forward with reserves of force that spring to her without effort; the will of the Titan is abstract and invents itself in a void. The forms the sculptor has made on her side are rich and sensuous; on the side of the Titan everything is tense with mental pride. Round the goddess the forms and figures are shaped by a calm and certain inner fullness, a force that has no need to hasten; the attendants of the Titan writhe away in doubt, in the complications of evasive thought. The goddess is raising her shaft against the Titan without any malice or even any sense of judgment. Her face— what a face, so young and beautiful—has the serene inward smile of wisdom and love. Her eyes look upward. They have no interest at all in the killing. They are turned toward the eternal.

This morning I looked hard at the Titan. The ruthlessness of unacknowledged despair has given him an animal head and a mockery of the human body. His head seems insolent until you really study it—then you see it is weighted down by its weariness. Helpless in an ill will now rounding upon itself, his repressed longing for liberation brings him face to face with her. He never meant to meet her; but he has come to the destined place. And she in her mercy has met his desperate dream in its own terms *to free him from it*. The killing will be a birth.

Peter used to keep a postcard of this sculpture on his writing desk.

love
Anna

I read Anna's letter over in various states of euphoria and depression. In those first three days in Rhodes my life too had shifted.

CHARLES TO ADOLPHE

Rhodes

Adolphe

Thanks for sending on Anna's letter. So she's taken up theogamy, has she? God knows she's been through almost everything else. All the boy with the turquoise bandana ever did for me was to row me downriver and charge me twenty rupees.

I'm sounding flat and bitter, but just at this moment—
in Rhodes, New York, in grayest midwinter—it is hard
to feel anything else. The wallpaper in this hotel does
not help—fat fading roses on baby blue. The basin is
chipped and a most unholy saffron; the curtains are
made of some greeny-orangey plastic stuff there can be
no decent name for. Another three days here, and I feel
I too would be sitting staring into space chewing or talking to myself like the old Negro in the lift, who goes up
and down in it all day for something to do, or pulling
angrily at my hair in the mirror like the waitress in the
hamburger joint down the road, whose eyes are still alive
enough to be bitter at what is being bled from them.

Richard isn't here.

You'd guessed that, I suppose.

I've looked everywhere—the Greek restaurant, the
Italian restaurant, the library, the chapel, the swimming
pool, the apartment block where he used to live . . . I've
walked up and down this town at all hours of the day
and night. I've stood at the Greyhound bus station amid
the gum wrappers and Diet Pepsi tins, watching people
coming off buses from Washington, Florida, Philadelphia.

"Aren't you goin' anywhere?" the man at the desk
asked me finally.

"Not yet."

"Are you crazy or somethin'?"

Sometimes in the street when I'm very tired I see Richard turning a corner—a back like his, his neck, his hair.
I shout out his name and run up to him. Another man
turns. I even spent an afternoon up at the old watch-
tower on the top of the hill, with a pair of hired binoc-
ulars. There was a drunk up there with me, lying with

his back to the window. "Never see nothing from up here, son. Never see nothing from up here." I rang up old acquaintances I hoped never to see again. "Have you seen Richard Hughes?" "But didn't he leave five years ago?" "Yes, of course. Of course he did." I spent a whole day at the top of the New Museum in the Eastern room, looking out over the snowy hills and waiting by the big Chinese goddess of compassion. After six hours or so, the old woman attendant brought me a ham sandwich. "You must be hungry from all that starin'."

The trail leads nowhere. Richard's probably in Miami, being blown by an heiress, getting a tan.

That's too vulgar an ending. Why should Richard have to pay even here for *my* fantasy? It was my vanity, my belief in my own powers of divination, that brought me here. Nothing to do with him.

What a pompous greedy manipulative fool I've been.

I believe the story of the man in Istanbul. I believe it because I saw it. Those forces exist. But why should I have imagined that I had earned the right to benefit by them? What have I done to deserve them? How could I have believed I had the right to ask them to work for me? And what did I really expect to find when I found Richard?

Do you want the truth? I wanted the tritest of things. *My* version of trite, of course — very Technicolor-tantric-spiritual-sexy. On the bus coming up here I composed three endings.

One: Richard would be waiting as I got off the bus. He would be wearing the blue jersey he wore when we first met. He would take me up to the waterfall, now frozen, where we often sat. We would lie in the snow and make love. We would have two visions, at least.

Two: The bus would be late. I would arrive in the middle of the night. All the hotels would be closed. I would walk the streets. Richard would be sitting in the piazza at the center of the shopping mall. He would be playing chess. We often played chess there. He would be waiting for me to move my pieces. I would go up to him, say nothing. He would look up and take my queen.

Then up to the waterfall.

Same as first.

Three: This version *begins* at the waterfall . . .

What am I to do with Richard's notebooks? By "do," I mean how to understand them? How to understand anything of what we each have been through . . . Have we all been mad from the beginning?

I'm going to sleep, Adolphe. I'm not going to finish this letter just yet.

All the plots that desire has spun in my life have been absurd. This one most of all. Which is not to say that desire is doomed. It may not be for others. But for me, for the work I must do, the path I must take . . . There I go again, categorizing, defining, confining.

I've just drawn the Tarot. I thought, why not ask it to interpret what is happening? Clearly the conscious Charles is about as much use as . . . I can't think of a useless enough analogy.

I shuffle and get

THE EMPRESS
JUSTICE
THE SUN

The Empress, with her scepter. Justice, with her sword (two women again!). The Sun. You know what the Sun looks like—two half-naked men, twins (and I a Gemini), putting their arms around each other. What optimistic cards? Who is joking with whom?

I can connect nothing with nothing and my finger-nails are both dirty and broken. I feel like flinging the cards out of the window. Calm. Maybe I'll understand in the morning.

If there is one thing I should have learnt by now, it is to keep open to new interpretations. How virtuous that sounds!

> Here lies Charles.
> Make reverent prostrations;
> For he was always open
> To new interpretations.

Next morning

The room is full of chill sunlight. I put on the radio today for the first time. By some sane miracle, it is Mozart's *Sinfonia Concertante,* the slow movement. The cards from last night's reading still face me:

> THE EMPRESS
> JUSTICE
> THE SUN

I stare at them, uncomprehending. Then I have the idea. I invite Adolphe and Anna in to interpret them. They are wiser than I. (Don't smile, and *don't* feel proud; almost anyone on this earth is wiser than I am.) You, Adolphe, swept in immediately.

"Well, it's obvious. She—the Empress—your muse, your psyche—brought you here to teach you a lesson. There she is, too, dressed up in drag, as Justice.

"The lesson is not too dolorous. It takes place under

the protection of the sun, *her* sun. Who are the two twins hugging each other? Not you and Richard. You are hugging your newly discovered sadder-wiser self. Haven't I often said, 'The greatest sex is with one's inner self'?"

Anna has come in by now and is standing by the door, watching both of us. She draws off her long black gloves and lays them along the cards. "No," she says. She is looking disgustingly well. She is looking like a fleshly version of the *Sinfonia Concertante*.

"No *what?*"

"Adolphe has got the interpretation wrong. The twins embracing each other *are* you and Richard—you and the real Richard, free at last of your fantasy."

I have probably misrepresented you both, as I have always misrepresented everything.

The light has changed to its favorite dull gray. How did I ever imagine anything magical and half-miraculous could happen in this postlapsarian arsehole?

Anna again: "It could. But *not to you.*"

It has started to snow.

I'll write once more from Antonia's . . .

> your chastened grandchild
> Charles

As I finish this I see Richard in my mind's eye, standing at the corner of a town square. It isn't anywhere we have been together, anywhere I recognize. Just a town like a thousand others somewhere in North America. He is eating a ham sandwich and looking calm and rather well. I do not have the feeling that he is thinking of me.

Paris

Darling Fool—

Sending you this Express to cheer you up and make you feel important again.

You've been *such* an ass, it's wonderful. What could that poor woman in the museum have thought, watching you wait by the goddess of whatsit? Don't you know that real goddesses are never in museums?

Don't you ever put *me* in a museum. I'd come alive and frighten people out of their jumpsuits.

Your portrayal of me interpreting the cards is *outrageously* dull-witted, but then *tant piss,* as my dear vulgar mother used to say. She also used to say, "I don't mind the piss being taken out of me, providing you put it back." That doesn't mean anything but it sounds marvelous.

I'm afraid to say I admit Anna's interpretation—damn her eyes; how dare you do this to me?—by far the smartest and harshest, so *bound* to be right.

As for what I find Abdul knew before—well, now *you* know it, or are beginning to. . . .

Enough of you and enough of that. *Much* more important things to talk about when you get back.

As for what to do about Richard's notebooks—why should you have been wrong about their insight and beauty simply because he didn't turn up to make love to you by a waterfall? Is it just possible that Richard has seen things *quite independent* of you—things you might learn from, be inspired by, along with the rest of us? For shame, pondy. Give the man his own notebooks at least. All the rest you can make over as you like, but leave him those.

God, you have got a lot to learn, and thank god I am here to teach you.

Adolphe

CHARLES TO ADOLPHE

Adolphe—

Your properly insulting letter arrived just in time. *This* part of the story is ended, anyhow.

Antonia is arriving tomorrow, so I have had to clean the flat. I am sitting here naked, hot, covered in fluff, ash, and dishwashing liquid. I must remember myself like this and never have pretensions again.

Richard's mother rang me yesterday morning. She told me that Richard had returned, "looking tanned and well," while I was away in Rhodes. I was so annoyed I forgot to ask where he had returned from. Then she said in her best Bostonian voice, "I trust you will send me a complete inventory of your expenses."

"You trust right."

After a few cagey generosities on both sides, we hung up. Richard rang an hour later.

"Charles, how are you?"

"How are *you?*"

"Very well."

Pause.

"It was good of you to come."

"I came for you."

Pause.

"I came for us, I mean."

Pause.

Richard cleared his throat. "I want you to know I am well and I regret having wasted your time." His voice sounded clear and decisive, like his father's. I had forgotten he had this voice. "Yes," he said, "things at home got a bit crazy, so I went up to Cape Cod to cool off. I worked on the fishing boats. You know how I love the sea. I feel great."

Pause.

"I'm glad."

Pause.

"How do you feel?"

"Oh, great."

"What was Rhodes like?"

"Great ... Your notebooks—what shall I do with them?"

Long pause. His voice came back with studied brightness. "They are trash. Trash I wrote when I was out of it. Keep them or send them, as you like."

I understood. Richard did not think his notebooks trash. He was afraid of them, and of what he had found out, seen, intuited. He wanted to leave them, their state of mind, and me behind. He had to if he was to live the life he wanted for himself—a life with limits, out of the wind of madness. Who was I to say he did not have the right to that life, on his terms? I had not felt the pain or exposure of madness or the kind of vision he had experienced. I did not have the right to demand he should be faithful to them or me. I had to allow him to give us both up.

He had given us up already. I had to allow *myself* to recognize that and to act on it.

So I said nothing.

Then Richard said, "Charles, you have been the best friend I have ever had. We'll see each other in Paris."

"Of course," I said, "you are welcome always where I am."

We waited a long time, listening to the wires hum between us. Richard needed me to say nothing, and he was waiting to see if I would, if I *could* be silent. I was silent. He put the phone down slowly.

I packed his notebooks. They are my right, I think. I am probably wrong even in that.

I'll hand you this letter when we meet, so you are up to date.

Charles

·FIVE·

"Up to date? Up to *date*? What a disgusting phrase."

Adolphe laughed and threw the letter down onto the small lacquer table in front of him. He looked frail and thin, but had underlined his eyes in red and purple and was wearing a bright blue silk robe with two gold dragons on it.

"Let me look at you," he said, taking my head in his hands. "A little baggy under the eyes. Too much of Antonia's vodka. But I thought you'd have that I-must-forsake-the-world look that you usually have when you have been defeated in love. Thank god you don't. One should never repeat oneself . . ."

His hands on my face were so thin and bony I shivered.

"Yes, pondy," he said, "it is the last lap now."

"Adolphe . . ."

"You must be at least as brave as I am being, although that will be hard. I know I look like a cross between a ladybird and a walrus at the moment, but you'll just have to bear it."

Winter sunlight fell over the room from the two large windows open onto Saint Sulpice. The murmur of voices and car horns came up to us.

"Yesterday," Adolphe said, "the fountain was frozen

231

over and de Cambray and Bossuet looked distinctly piqued. But today, now you are here, the water is dancing again."

The bell on the great white door rang.

"That'll be Abdul. He's bringing something for you."

"A present?"

"You should have seen the way your eyes lit up when you said that. Never lose greed. It keeps you young."

Abdul swaggered in, sweating from his climb up the spiral stairs, but almost imperial in a vast swaying tent of a black cashmere overcoat covered with medals.

"He's wearing his medals," Adolphe whispered to me. "Not always a good sign. Do you know Abdul has been decorated by more governments than Errol Flynn?"

"I heard that," said Abdul, wiping his brow. "Why is it you always mock my courage?" He said *courage* "cowerage," very long and drawn out. "I have the V.C., the Légion d'Honneur—"

"Abdul, no boasting," said Adolphe. He turned to me. "Isn't it ridiculous, Charles, that after all Abdul and I have been through, we should still behave like two pantomime dwarfs whenever we meet?"

"*Dwarfs!*" bellowed Abdul. "*Dwarfs!*" He drew himself up to his full immense size and flexed his biceps. The medals shook and trembled. Then he swept across the room and enfolded Adolphe in his black cashmere arms.

Adolphe disentangled himself. "I'm not sure which is worse, your medals or your Turkish Delight hugs."

Abdul sat smiling and picking his teeth.

"Have you got what I asked for?" demanded Adolphe.

Abdul pointed to a small gold plastic bag he had left by the door. "It is in there. And I have brought music too. But first I must tell you about my *Portia fimbriata*."

"Another of the Italian heiresses you go in for?"

"I haven't been 'in for' Italian heiresses for at least ten years. And when I was in for them I always won." He played his fat fingers up and down his medals.

"Who is this Portia?" I asked in my "tactful" voice. "Have I met her?"

Abdul grinned, flaunting his gold caps. "No, you have never met her. Or you have, but in another disguise."

Abdul reached into the small left-hand pocket of his cashmere and drew something out of it.

Adolphe screamed, "*Oh my god oh my god!*"

"Don't be so stupid. Anyone would think you were a schoolgirl seeing a spider for the first time. Now say hello to Portia, Charles and Adolphe, and stop all this." A tiny brown spider lay in Abdul's palm. "It is not dead. I gave it a little hashish in water before I came out."

"Since she can't now speak for herself," Adolphe said, "do you think you could introduce her? Semiformally, of course."

Abdul closed his eyes. "You think I have just brought her here for entertainment. Oh you of little faith! Oh my sadly skeptical children! How much longer must you wander in the forests of unknowing!"

"No preliminaries necessary, Abdul. Where does Portia come from?"

"The rainforests of Queensland."

"No pun intended, I hope. Remember whom you are amongst."

"I have no prejudices," Abdul said grandly. "Everything, except for dogs and little children, is permitted in my carnal universe."

"But from *Australia,* Abdul!"

"Yes, Australia—the oldest and the newest place. The most ancient, and that continent in which . . . No more; there are things even you cannot know."

"Abdul is very grandiose today."

"There are days, my dear Adolphe, when being grandiose is the only possible response. I shall unveil to you the miracle of *Portia fimbriata*. And you will become aware, if you have half a brain, of how much she has to teach us." Abdul stood up and looked round the room as if to see where he should position himself. With a grunt he chose the Buddha from Siam in the right-hand corner. "Most spiders," he began, "belong to one of two broad groups, the sedentary web builders and the running, jumping hunters. Web builders have poor vision generally; they detect their insect prey by the vibrations of their web. Jumpers do not as a rule build webs. They hunt their prey on vegetation or open ground. The other important thing about them—salticids, as they are called—is that they have highly developed vision."

"Abdul, I know all this," said Adolphe plaintively. "I'm dying to be told what I *don't* know."

Abdul cleared his throat. "Well, I bet you don't know this. Portia is both. Both a web builder and a jumping spider. Now do you see?"

"See what?"

"What she has to teach us? We must run and hunt and jump for the true and beautiful. We must have razor-sharp vision, preferably 360 degrees, like hers; grow all six celestial eyes if necessary; and we must also build webs. And we must also learn from Portia the cryptic rest posture."

"The what?"

Abdul repeated patiently, "The cryptic rest posture. When Portia is being hunted, she masks the outline of her legs and palps by flexing them and holding them close to the body. The hair fringes on the legs and tufts on the abdomen help to make Portia look like a leaf."

"Quite a program," Adolphe said.

"Yes, and not much time to accomplish it in," said Abdul.

Adolphe smiled. "First dolphins, then hummingbirds, then ants, and now—"

"*Portia fimbriata*," Abdul completed. "For we are both entering, my brother, the stage of the cryptic rest posture."

There was a sudden silence, broken at last by a slight high cough from Adolphe. "But I have no hair on my legs and no sweet disguising tufts on my abdomen."

"Don't be *literal*."

Abdul came and sat down on the sofa again, putting Portia back into the cashmere pocket with a soft "Sleep there and dream, little one, *babushka mia*."

"Aren't you mixing up your languages a bit?"

"Portia mixes up all categories. Why should I not mix languages? Out of the mix shall come forth the New One."

"What sacred text is that from?"

"The Evangel of Abdul. Composed but not yet written. There are some other things that might excite you about Portia—excite and instruct. You, Anna, and Charles," he said, "could be one of her webs."

"Don't go floaty, Abdul."

"The webs built by Portia generally consist of three inclined sheets converging at the bottom and opening at the top." Abdul got up off the sofa and started to dance the Charleston. Adolphe and I looked on with fear. He gave a whoop and then stopped, flopping back next to Adolphe and mopping his brow.

"Is that sort of exercise good for you?" remarked Adolphe acidly.

"Leave me out of it. Don't you see? Don't you *SEE*?

You, Anna, and Charles—the three sheets, converging at the bottom . . ."

"And opening at the top. Thank you, Abdul, we *had* got it."

Abdul looked crestfallen. "No," he said brightly, "I am *not* going to sulk. Whatever the provocation, I am not going to sulk."

Adolphe stroked his right arm. "I'm sorry, my sweet Abdul . . . Can Portia really see 360 degrees?"

"Yes," came Abdul's voice, small and rather tearful.

"How marvelous and inspiring." Adolphe sounded very sincere.

"And we all are going to try to become her," said Abdul.

"Abdul, that *is* asking . . ." Adolphe turned to me. "See what I have been putting up with since you went away? Every day, almost, Abdul finds another miraculous species and I have to swear to try to become it. Otherwise he gets *very* angry. For Abdul there are no earthly limits. Now, Abdul, read Charles's last letter. It's very funny. Catch up on the Saga of Charles while I go and open that plastic bag." He handed Abdul the letter and walked over to the plastic bag. Suddenly he fell. "Oh my god," he said softly, clutching his left side.

I ran to where he lay in a pile of blue silk.

"Don't touch me. I must get up on my own. I *must*. Sometimes I feel I have no limbs left. I say to my leg, 'Move,' and it isn't there. Enough of that. Sometimes I think my legs and arms are as large as Paris. I feel I am a huge balloon that covers Paris, and everything going on is going on inside me. That fountain over there, I feel it trickling down the sides of the balloon . . . Enough of *that* too." Adolphe dusted down his silk sleeves. "How do I look? Fetching?" His face had aged ten years in the fall. His eyes were sunken and full of pain. Only his voice was strong.

I could not say anything.

"Go on. Lie a little. Marlene always says, 'Lie truthfully enough and your lie will become truth.' But then she is German, after all."

"You look—" I began.

"I look," he said, "like an old plastic doll left too close to the fire. But then, I was never a beauty, so why should I care? Yet one does so want to be radiant in one's coffin, doesn't one? Like Duse, with masses of false hair and flowers." He giggled. "I'm going to be embalmed in white honey, like Alexander the Great."

"You are *not*," growled Abdul.

"Abdul is such a puritan. I'm going to be embalmed and put on display in Saint Sulpice. Alexander wore white silk shorts, and so will I."

"*Silk shorts*, Adolphe?"

"Well, not shorts, darling, Kashmir pajamas. The kind that cover a multitude of sins." Adolphe was standing by the plastic bag now. "Come here, Charles. I have something for you." I went and stood by him. We looked down at the bag together. "It's come all the way from Sanjusangendo . . . and across forty years."

"Sanjusawhere?"

He repeated the name slowly, raptly. "Sanjusangendo. It is a holy place of Japan. I visited it first before the war. It has a temple with a covered gallery. The gallery has a thousand life-sized statues in it of the goddess Kwannon, goddess of compassion. Each statue has twelve arms. Twelve! More even than Kali . . . More than Durga, than Saraswati . . . twelve arms forming a breast-high corolla, a sunburst as golden as the halo around her head . . . Each statue is the same, but totally different, just as the same note played successively changes in the time you listen to it. In a dream last week I saw the gallery again. This time the statues were also mirrors, mirrors that rotated slowly in different times to a quiet music of bells. In each of the turning mirrors all the others were reflected, all the other haloes of arms, and smiles . . . I looked quite marvelous, although I say it myself. I was in my white Schiaparelli, you know, the one she made for Mrs. Reginald Fellowes. Perfection! Close your eyes."

"*Adolphe*—"

"Close your eyes. It is required that you awaken your faith. And sit down cross-legged on the floor."

"Adolphe, I'm just back from New York, City of Skepticism."

"Close your eyes."

I closed my eyes, and heard Adolphe walking across the room to the windowsill where he keeps his records and record player.

The music began. It was unlike any I had ever heard. It began with a few random soundings of bells, very light, and as if from a great distance. Then a drum came in, quietly and evenly. Slowly other bells joined in with the ones already sounding, in an asymmetric, arhythmic way that was yet more ordered than any music I had ever heard—ordered at a different level of awareness. It was a music without violence of any kind and without grief, yet with a great weight as well as lightness, a severity that derived from the clarity of the ring of the bells and the hollow ringing spaces between their sounding.

As I listened, dreamlike images formed in my mind. I saw a pool of water, calm at first, surrounded by tall

238

trees in their autumn gold. Slowly from the center of the pool a vibration began, a ripple that became a circle of water and light that seemed in its rhythmic trembling at once to create the music and be created by it. The pool grew calm again, as unruffled as a mirror. I looked to see if the trees were reflected in it. They were not. Nothing, not even the small light clouds in the sky, was reflected in it. Slowly, as the music grew louder again, a face appeared in the mirror. First a headdress of brilliant feathers; then the hair, braided and golden; finally, as the drums deepened and the bells chimed together, the smile, the smile of Kwannon. The water seemed to catch fire around it . . .

"You can open your eyes now." Adolphe's voice came from very far away, but when I opened my eyes he was sitting cross-legged facing me. He had drawn the curtains of the flat and lit seven candles round him. He had changed his blue silk gown, and now wore a simple black kimono. He placed a small object in front of me, with the plastic bag folded over it to hide it. He fixed me with his eyes and said, "You can take off the cover now."

I raised the plastic cover. Immediately Adolphe laughed and blew out all the candles.

"I can't see anything."

"Wait."

I waited, looking down into the dark space where the object was. I stared, but nothing was visible, not even the Buddhas in the corners. I shifted from leg to leg. The room suddenly seemed cold.

"Do you need some more music?" Adolphe's voice was mocking.

"I'm being patient. What more can I do?"

Then I saw it, quite clearly, as if in broad daylight.

It was a miniature garden.

It was a miniature of the place Georges Cain, but with all the trees tiny, gnarled, and Japanese. And surrounded not by the street or the iron railing but by a pool. The center of the garden was not the baroque Flora but a tiny Kwannon, holding up in her right hand a mirror. At first when I saw the garden I wanted to laugh. At first glance it looked absurdly gnarled and bijou and artificial. Some wiser instinct stopped me, thank god, because as I looked at it I saw the three of us in it, Anna, myself, and Adolphe. We were walking as we had walked that evening those weeks ago.

I have the feeling as I write that *if I had laughed* I would have killed us in the garden. There we were in miniature, but *alive* . . . Anna was dressed in a black evening dress, I in a robe of some sort, Adolphe in his white Schiaparelli . . .

"Oh my god," I said.

Anna, Adolphe, and I were opening the gate of the garden. The mirror of Kwannon was flashing a white light to every part of the garden—long silken strands of white light. We were opening the gate and walking towards the water.

I became frightened. Adolphe gripped my arm. "It is all right. Do not worry. Do not be afraid."

In the miniature garden, Anna, Adolphe, and I were at the edge of the water. We reached out to each other and held each other's hands. We were obviously intoning something to one another, but what it was I could not hear. Where we were standing, the water became dark and turbulent.

"No," I said.

"Yes," Adolphe said, putting his hand over my mouth. "Yes. Yes, you fool."

At Adolphe's yes, very loud, the water calmed down and furrows appeared on it. It was as if the water was a plowed field. The tops of the furrows were lined with the white light from the flashing mirror.

"Walk in the middle," Adolphe said beside me.

And the three started to walk in the middle of different furrows across the water . . .

Adolphe laughed and slowly lit the seven candles. I closed my eyes. When I opened them, I cried out.

The miniature garden was just a miniature garden. It was nothing but a Japanese miniature garden with the usual dumb sage sitting on a bench under a willow. And three dirty-looking stones by his feet.

Adolphe bent over, licked his little finger, and rubbed the stones. "The packing is never satisfactory."

"But, Adolphe—"

"Shut up for once. We'll disturb Abdul."

I looked round. The curtains were open and the room full of light. Abdul was watching us, my letter lying by his feet.

"I didn't know, Adolphe, you were—"

"*No words.* Besides, I'm not. The power is elsewhere. A good present, don't you think?" He looked exhausted again.

I leaned forward to stroke his forehead. He recoiled. "No pity. I'm going in the way I want to. I'm burning out and flowing out and that is what I have always prayed for. In these last days there must be no grief. We've both done enough grieving in our time for several lifetimes."

Abdul coughed behind us. "What a pompous thing to say. Enough grieving for several lifetimes. What about *me?* Did I not lose my parents in Smyrna? Did my Corinthia not betray me with the Mexican ambassador? *The*

Mexican ambassador." Abdul beat his breast operatically.

"Was the ambassador handsome?"

"As Tyrone Power. And had a long silken black moustache, with which, I am told—no, no obscenities. His name was Luis. I had my revenge. I named a tarantula after him. A *female* tarantula, to make it more shameful."

Adolphe and I went to sit with Abdul on the sofa.

"So what, Abdul," Adolphe asked, "did you think of Charles's saga?"

"To tell you frankly," Abdul said, "my frankness, which is legendary in the business circles of several continents—"

"Out with it."

"To tell you frankly, I was disappointed." Abdul grinned at being so disappointed.

"What do you mean, disappointed? That is what happened," I said.

"That is what I mean, you fool," Abdul said. "You see, I keep hoping for Reality to break into flame and illumine the world, but it never quite seems to."

"Let us be honest," said Adolphe in a quiet voice. "*Completely* honest. Charles deserves it."

Abdul and Adolphe glanced at each other, bowed slightly, braced their shoulders, and started to speak together.

"I think it should be you who says it," Abdul said. "For Charles's purposes, I'm just an exotic accessory."

I began to protest.

"My dear Charles, being an exotic accessory is something I have done very well all my life. I'm delighted to be useful once again. Why would I ever have bought this coat four sizes too big had I not been determined to be picturesque?"

Adolphe walked to the window. He turned and stared at me.

"Why are you staring like that?" I asked him.

"I'm searching your face for clues as to how I should begin."

"Just begin," I said exasperatedly. "I've never known you to beat about the bush."

"To be quite frank, Charles," Adolphe began, "Abdul and I both think your web stinks."

"You are mixing your metaphors."

"Don't be clever. This is not the time." There was something alarmingly cold in Adolphe's voice.

"Adolphe—"

"Charles, sit down and listen."

I sat down on the floor.

"The web must be changed," Adolphe said grimly.

"Don't be absurd, Adolphe. I can't change it. That is how it happened. Those are the facts. In my letters I wrote nothing but the facts."

Adolphe shouted, "Never ever call me absurd in that superior Oxford voice of yours! You may terrify your students and your parents and the boys you lug off the streets, but you will never *ever* frighten me. Understood?" He came over to where I was sitting and stood over me. "Don't you understand anything yet?"

"How can I change my web, as you call it—"

"Look, Charles, *you* spun the web. Your will, your fantasy. It didn't just *happen*. *You* made choice after choice, some conscious, some only half so, and what happened arose out of your choices. *See* the web as it is, as you made it. If you don't, you will be trapped in what you yourself have spun. It will be a wheel on which you turn—"

243

"And burn," said Abdul.

"And burn. Don't you see, Charles, throughout your quest for Richard you were still caught in your old fantasy of fulfillment? You wanted to improvise, and play with, the past; you still hoped against hope, admit it, for some unexpected utopian ending, some *Tristan und Isolde* resolution. You wanted to play the sage, the saint, the lover, the psychiatrist, all in one. And then your desires started naturally to write the plot. God, how you wrote it, feverishly, missing every clue.

"You continued spinning your petty little web while here a new dimension altogether was being entered and explored. I could have written that I had changed completely into a diamond or a hummingbird, or started to walk on the Seine in the afternoons; you would have written back, 'I'm so happy for you, Adolphe. Now listen to what Richard writes . . .'"

"Please—"

"What makes the whole thing sadder and stranger is that you were for seconds partially aware of other possibilities. But you misinterpreted them, or rather you interpreted them as making *you* the center of things, the architect of destiny. Instead of being doors through which you could walk, they became counters you could use, strands you could bind your wretched web with." Adolphe sank onto the sofa.

"But Richard . . . ," I said helplessly.

"*Richard?*" Adolphe shouted. "Don't you see that Richard was blank enough for you to project anything you wanted on him? Why did he go mad in the first place? Because he was vulnerable to *your* fantasy, able to enter it almost completely. Richard's psyche and yours wrote the web together. And the web ended when he signed off. Which suited you."

"Suited me?"

"Oh, Charles, surely you are not *that* naive? What would you have done if he really had been waiting in that upstairs room by the goddess of compassion? Perhaps if you *had* wanted it enough, it would have happened. Those things can happen. But you didn't *want* it. Because if it *had* happened, you would have lost yourself. You would have had to *merge* with Richard, lose your separateness in him.

"You write of making love by the waterfall. But you would *never* have done that. You would have found a way out of ecstasy at the last moment. You would have noticed his aftershave, or contrived to slip on a rock, or suddenly gone limp *in medias res*. No, Richard's signing off was perfect for you. It gave you a finite structure. It gave you that ball of grief you need to spin your plots out of. It gave you the sense of superiority you love. Don't deny a *word* of what I have been saying. And don't feel *guilty*, otherwise your guilt will spin yet another illusion. And don't look bruised. We are all stupid. But you are very intelligent as well as stupid, which makes you a very hard nut to crack. All puns intended."

"So all the time you were writing your marvelous letters . . ."

"I was watching to see how you would spin."

"You bastard."

Adolphe laughed. "I prefer it when you're angry. You don't look bruised. But you're not going to *stay* angry, are you? That would be very unintelligent."

Abdul coughed. "May I interpose something?"

"Interpose? You've never used that word before."

245

"I try to use a new word every day. Yesterday it was *sesquipedalian*." Abdul stood up, stroking his stomach. "Everything you say, Adolphe, is true. But I want to go back to what I was saying."

"What a surprise," Adolphe whispered.

"I heard that," said Abdul. "But I forgive everything."

"I want to say something," I said suddenly. "If I hadn't spun that web I wouldn't be here listening to you unpicking it. I had to live out my folly to have a chance of seeing it clearly."

Adolphe paused, and then said, "I hoped you weren't going to say that."

"Why?"

"I wanted you to squirm slightly for a bit. Just a bit. I wanted you not to suffer exactly, but to *squirm*. But now you've found me out." He was smiling. "Just because your complex stupidity and concupiscence brought you *here*, that's no reason—"

"Yes it is," interrupted Abdul. "He must bless even his silliest features. You cannot transform, Adolphe, what you cannot bless."

"Abdul, the wisdom that sings out of you today—"

"Is like the singing of the bulbul in my grandmother's garden. Yes." Abdul sighed. "On occasion I can be wonderfully wise. It is true. I even surprise myself sometimes. There it is—wisdom—in a phrase, a gesture, floating out of me towards others . . ." Abdul's vision of his own wisdom so contented him that he sat back on the sofa and closed his eyes. Then he opened them again. "I nearly forgot what I wanted to say. There is only one thing that truly disappointed me in Charles's story. I bet you can't imagine what it was."

Abdul looking roguish is not a pretty sight.

246

"Go on," said Adolphe warily.

"It is to do with a waterfall," he said coyly.

"Oh, Abdul, you old romantic. You wanted them to . . . to . . ."

"Yes," breathed Abdul. "Yes. I hoped that Charles's psyche would allow him sexual ecstasy. But, as you have already said, Adolphe, Charles flirts with ecstasy but always chooses solitude. This must *change*. This is the Old Consciousness. Full of perceptions, even a certain kind of wry awareness, but very *foutu*. *Foutu* was the word of the day before yesterday. Oh, I was hoping for quite another end to the story, the most daring, anarchic end."

"Abdul—"

"Don't stop me. I have my flights and floods too, my friend, and I feel very sesquipedalian in spirit at this moment."

"My lord," said Adolphe, "I've never seen him quite this excited. It must be sexual."

"Of course it is sexual," said Abdul very grandly. "And why shouldn't it be? You're not a puritan, by any chance? Be anything, my dear, but a puritan. Life is not a music to be composed in G minor."

"I said that first," said Adolphe.

"I steal yours and you steal mine. That is one way in which we become each other. You also said once, 'The goal of life is to be excessive in C major.' You were in trance at the time, listening to sitar music. But I copied it into my notebook and used it on several occasions. Amazing what a musical reference can do, you know."

"Will you stop this?" I intervened.

"Can't bear it when we turn away from *you*, can you?"

"I'm just anxious—"

"To steal what I am about to say, to incorporate it into

247

your web—why not? You could do worse. I have spun well in my time and my strands are good-quality Middle Eastern silk, hard as nails and soft as a baby's bottom."

"I said that too," said Adolphe complacently.

"Will you stop that?" said Abdul. "Surely now all our voices are one? What do you think about that, Charles? Are all our voices one or not?"

I suddenly felt a wave of very ordinary jet lag sweep over me.

"If you say so, Abdul."

"I don't want you to accept things just because I say so. Yes I do, come to think of it. But this is carrying us far from what my friends the Americans would call the sexual area."

"I have never heard any American say 'the sexual area,'" I said sulkily.

"Quite clearly we have moved in different social circles. Let me just ask you plainly. Why didn't you make tantric love by the waterfall?"

"Abdul," I began patiently, "you have read the letters. Richard wasn't there."

"That is a very *realist* explanation and as such limited."

"Baudelaire wrote somewhere," I said, "'on the higher slopes of love, you need conspirators.' Richard wasn't a conspirator, that's all. It takes two to tantra." I looked to Adolphe for a smile. He looked up at the ceiling, rolling his eyeballs.

Abdul came to me and took my hands. "You really must stop being clever. You must dive, my friend. There are pearls, Rumi wrote, but you must dive for them."

"*You* wrote that, Abdul," said Adolphe. "Rumi would have put it better."

"Okay, I wrote it. It's true, whoever wrote it. My dear

Charles, you could never have made love by that water-fall because you never really believed you could. You have to dream reality before it can happen. You have to dream the future before it can materialize. The dream must be as large and open and amazing and anarchic as possible. Only then can reality change. Am I making myself clear?"

"Clearish," I said, "but you seem sometimes to be speaking in German."

"I think I ought to step in here," said Adolphe jealously.

Adolphe does not like Abdul to appear too authoritative.

"There is a poem by Basho," Adolphe began.

"With you," I said, "there is always a poem by Basho."

Adolphe went into his bedroom and returned with a large black piece of paper on which he wrote in great white letters:

Unknown spring
Plum blossom
Behind the mirror

"I haven't the slightest idea what it means," I said stolidly.

"That is the problem," Adolphe murmured. "Try harder." He recited it out loud, savoring each word:

Unknown spring
Plum blossom
Behind the mirror

"How can it be unknown—" I began.

"If it is behind the mirror?" interrupted Adolphe. "Or if he knows, in some sense, that it is behind the mirror?

Exactly. It is both known and unknown, guessed at and not quite attained. The rapture is real, but always on the other side of the mirror. But that does not mean it cannot communicate. It can, but always from this mysterious distance, across this strange barrier."

"Now *you* are speaking in German," I said.

"These things are difficult, you cuttlefish. They can't just be said pat-pat."

"But what has it got to do with 'the sexual area'?"

Adolphe sighed. "Sometimes I wonder why I bother."

"You bother because you love me and because you know that I listen."

"Those are as good reasons as I can come up with." Adolphe smiled. "Now I want to tell you my vision. It has to do with lovely young butch gopis and Krishna."

"Adolphe," I explained carefully, "the gopis were women."

"That is just the sort of reactionary balls we have to get rid of. There were—are—male gopis too. Some of them even in drag." Adolphe did a very stately and elegant pirouette. "The vision happened during an afternoon nap, after reading *The Life of Hummingbirds*. I wasn't feeling sexy, just limitless. I found myself by the side of a forest clearing, dressed in nothing but a purple lungi. It was a musky, aromatic, warm night, and the clearing was lit with flickering torches, whose smoke smelt of sandalwood.

"In the middle of the clearing stood an Indian youth of the most stunning beauty, quite naked. It was Krishna. He was leaning with his hands on his hips, as in the statues. What hips, darling, slim and burnished. Around him—quite, quite naked also—were at least a hundred young men, almost as beautiful. They were all ... doing ... what they were doing ... with absolute, shameless, laughing abandon. Krishna stood smiling; they worshiped him with their . . . with their . . . use your imagination! I daren't describe it, I'd be struck by lightning. I'm not sure your repressed little libido could stand it.

"I was being shown, pondy, that the homosexual *eros* is just as holy as the male-female one, just as divine. The energy that was bursting and throbbing and jerking through the bodies of those gorgeous young men was the central energy, Krishna's energy, the energy of creation. The young men had exactly the same look of high abandon and shyness as the women gopis do in those Indian paintings of them, the same intoxicating mixture of tenderness and madness. Why did I not get all this sexy wisdom earlier? Why was there no one to tell me these things when I started my odysseys in the Bois de Boulogne and the Tuileries? Why was I shown the god and his gopis when I am a bag of cholesterol and cancer? What a gopi was lost in me! I never had a *real* gift for self-hatred and guilt: I could have goped with the best of them. It's up to you, up to you now, and yours . . . Get into that aromatic clearing quick and strip off! 'With my body I thee gope' . . . It doesn't have to be a great body, either. I was dancing with the others by the end, wearing my lungi as a turban, wobbling and juddering away . . ."

I began to laugh. Adolphe pretended to look offended.

"Here I am, revealing to you mysteries you should have had to do ten years' meditation in the snow for, and you laugh."

"You must admit—"

"Never apologize; never admit; never explain. My Irish nanny drummed that into me. There are vast treasures of wisdom and union stored in the secret places of sex. We must tunnel to them. I'm getting excited. I'm mixing my metaphors like billio—"

"You know," Abdul interrupted, "at the end, with my wife . . . it was . . . it was holy. She was old and fat; I was old and fat. But we *were* each other and we had no shame."

Abdul's simplicity made us all pause.

"What you talk of is not just for Krishnas and gopis," Abdul said. "It is for all of us if we can learn to give without fear."

"Heavens, dear Abdul," said Adolphe, "I never knew you felt so strongly."

"I've often told you, my dear, but you weren't listening."

"I apologize."

Abdul took Adolphe's hand.

"And," I began slowly, "what are you talking of, Adolphe, the union, the delight, the dance, is not only sexual . . ." Something wonderful was becoming clear. "You and I, Adolphe, for instance . . ." I looked at him; his face was very open and wrinkled. He was looking back at me calmly. The light in the room was a gentle early afternoon light. "Our souls have made love," I went on. "This is the tantra of friendship."

"Yes," Adolphe said, and turned to Abdul. "He's learning at last . . ."

Adolphe paused.

"I have felt it with you too, Abdul—when not diverted by irritations—the tenderness that shamelessly dissolves all barriers."

"And I with you." Abdul's medals heaved and shimmered.

"And I with Anna," Adolphe said. "God knows, we mustn't leave her out of it."

"And I with Anna," I said.

There was a long silence.

"Unknown spring," Adolphe began. "Unknown spring / Plum blossom / Behind the mirror."

He looked from Abdul to me, and clapped his hands. "And now, it's time to eat. First plum blossoms, then food. I'm dying of hunger. Now I'm dying I can really let myself go."

The phone rang at eight o'clock the next morning.

"I've got jet lag, Adolphe, do you realize . . ."

"Don't be *realist*. A letter from Anna has just arrived. *Her* web is much more revealing than either of ours. Thank god the two of us are in it too."

"What on earth are you babbling about?" I said, rubbing my eyes.

"It can't have escaped even your attention that Anna has been on a Great Trek. Well, she has reached bivouac."

"Don't be fancy, Adolphe. Tell me—"

But he had already put the phone down.

I showered, dressed, and was about to leave for Saint Sulpice when I heard the concierge's sharp double knock at my door. Madame Ermine had come to complain, as usual—about her eyes, her legs, the antics of her schizoid son ("The *flics* found him last night naked under a bridge, pretending to be Napoleon. Just like this time last year"). After her tirade she produced from her greasy pink apron a letter.

From America. From Richard.

She held it up, sniffed it, and said with a wink, "Pas de parfum."

"Quel dommage."

A letter from Richard so soon made me nervous.

When Madame Ermine left, I made some coffee and sat looking at the letter on my desk a long time before opening it. With a start I realized that I had placed it in exactly the same position as the letter from Richard's mother two months ago.

Then I thought, have I ever received a letter from Richard without being afraid?

Damn the fear. I opened it.

Charles—

I wasn't completely honest with you the last time we talked on the phone.

While I was away in Cape Cod I got married. To Carla, Susan's friend. Remember Carla? We had dinner together once in Rhodes. She's the small Jewish one with bright eyes and reddish hair. You argued about Milton's Eve. She thought Eve a sap and you did your spiel on Eve's spiritual beauty. She remembers you clearly.

It was not a sudden decision. I've been seeing her off and on for about two years. She has loved me patiently. It seems everyone has to love me patiently. I hope with her I shall give more than I have in the past. Part of the reason I ran off to Cape Cod was to marry her. Neither Mother nor Father approves. They think Carla vulgar and not "up to me." I feel like saying, "At least she is not black, or a man." (!)

Carla's parents gave us two thousand dollars for our wedding present. (They like me and know nothing about the past. I think they think I am the model wasp son-in-law, rather quiet, with bookish tastes.) Carla and I have decided that we are coming to Paris. Won't it be wonderful to be together, the three of us, in that city you have so often told me about, but which I have never seen? I feel strong enough at last for Paris, and open enough, with Carla beside me.

Is your apartment big enough for us to stay in? Two thousand dollars sounds a lot, but we intend to travel. Carla is into women's studies, and we want to travel all over Europe studying how women cope. Carla is a very committed person, full of ideas and visions. I think she is just about the most courageous person I have ever met.

I'm enclosing a photograph Carla took of me. I like it best of all my photographs.

I love you. You will always be, you know, the person that in my way I love most.

Richard

I buried my head in my hands, and then started to laugh. The photograph Richard had sent me of himself would have graced the centerfold of a soft-porn gay magazine. He was half naked, bronzed, smiling at the viewer (Carla!) from under a sunlit tilted white hat. He was standing with his legs provocatively apart and his right hand tucked into the top of his shorts.

I went and stood by the window and saw exactly what would happen if Carla and Richard came. I saw the tense brittle evenings at La Cafetière (which I would end up paying for); I saw Richard trying to catch my glance seductively when Carla had left the room; I saw Carla (I remembered her lank hair and green gimlet eyes clearly) clamping her legs together, watching us both . . . For a moment I was tempted to go through with it, to fight Carla for Richard, to play my part . . .

"*No*," I said out loud. "No. Not this time."

"Richard," I wrote carefully, and, for once, legibly,

What a sexy photograph.

Don't worry about the dishonesty. Good luck with the happiness.

I remember Carla equally clearly. I do not think we are destined to appreciate each other. My fault, no doubt.

I cannot invite you to Paris, as I am going to India soon for an indefinite period.

I think you know how much luck I wish you both.

Love
Charles

I remembered the Cartier ring Adolphe had given me to give Richard, before I set out for the States. I had taken it with me, and brought it back. Now, at last, I'd found a purpose for it. I sent it with the letter, for Richard to give to Carla.

I don't know what prompted me to write "I am going to India"; perhaps I felt a lie would be kinder than the full truth.

Sealing the letter with the ring in it and walking to post it in the rue des Saints Pères, I knew that I was at last letting Richard go, at last really losing him. That grieved me. It was the end of our story, a shabby unromantic end too. But ending it like this would free him as well as me. His fantasy of me as the perfect friend, ideal buddy, was in its way as vain as mine of him as the ideal lover, and rooted in as silly a selection of the evidence. Our illusions had often put us both in danger; it was time to try to end them.

I posted the letter; stopped off at the Flore for two stiff Pernods; walked in the freezing winter wind to Adolphe's. On the way I passed a young man who looked so like Richard that I had to stop and lean against a shop window.

"What renunciation! St. Francis himself . . ."

"Adolphe, please."

256

"I mean it, axolotl. I'm almost proud of you. I know how hard it is for you to give up any chance of a good complicated plot, with lots of suffering in it. Why don't you change your mind? Just ask them to come for a month? That is all you'd need for a real savage little romp."

I got one of Adolphe's purple silk cushions and threw it at him. He ducked nimbly. "I think you are very mean. *You* may not want to see Carla again, but you are quite wrong in assuming that I don't want to meet her. I love the Carlas of this world. They are charmless to the point of sublimity, and I adore challenges. As for Richard . . ."

"Stop it. I'm still feeling bruised."

"I should bloody well hope you are." Adolphe's tone was suddenly serious. "*Quite* enough of you. Anna's letter."

He spread the thin blue paper on the sofa in front of him.

It was then that I noticed the coffin—long, black, red-velvet–lined, and standing upright by the Buddha of Siam.

"What is *that?*"

"Darling, that is a stupid question even by your standards." Adolphe minced over to the coffin and stood in it. "How do I look?"

"Get out of there at once."

"Don't be such a spoilsport. I'm going to lie in it for a long while. I might as well get the feel of it. Bernhardt lay in hers every day for twenty minutes."

"Come out *at once.*"

"What severity. And you haven't even noticed."

"Noticed what?"

"The lining."

"Of course I've noticed the lining. It's red. Velvet."

"What kind of red?"

I looked blank.

"*Tibetan* red. Everything has to be explained to you . . . Hand me Anna's letter."

"What for?"

"I'm going to read it to you."

"Standing there?"

"Why not? If only I had thought of Coffy before. Think of meeting producers for my films in this! Why does one think of everything too late?"

"Please, Adolphe."

"No. Why should you steal the scene today, with your renunciation? I must have my splendors too."

I handed him Anna's letter. He put his right hand round the side of "Coffy" and a light went on above his head.

"A reading light. For the long winter evenings."

"Adolphe, you're becoming . . ."

"Morbid? No. Practical."

Adolphe was dressed in a black cocktail dress with a simple swept-back *soignée* black wig. As he began to read Anna's letter I understood why. He was *being* Anna. His voice, his way of holding his hands and of looking up quizzically after every sentence—these were Anna to the life, uncannily, eerily Anna. More than once as he was reading I closed my eyes to see whether I could tell Adolphe's Anna voice and my memory of Anna's voice apart. His was a little higher-pitched, but only marginally.

"'Dearest Adolphe and Charles,'" he began, adding as Adolphe, "It's postmarked Pondicherry, by the way." He put down the letter. "Are you ready for this?" he said. "Am I?"

"What are you talking about?"

"You'll see."

The phone rang.

"It'll be Abdul . . . Hello, Abdul. You can't come? You've just heard from the Tibetan? You know where he is? In the catacombs of Paris? How original! We'll go tonight. Of course. Come here about six."

"What was *that*?"

"I'll tell you later. Now for Anna's marvelous, miraculous letter."

"Get on with it."

Adolphe stuck out his tongue at me, and then began.

> My dearest friends, I have news that will complete and transform *this* stage of each of our lives.

"My god." I groaned. "Anna's being sibylline. I hope India doesn't burn away her sense of humor."

Adolphe started. He went on reading from Anna's letter:

> Sorry to be sibylline. You will see why in a moment. And don't worry: India has not burned away my sense of humor.

Adolphe put his hands on his hips. "If you don't believe she wrote those words, come and see for yourself." He brandished the letter from his coffin. I walked over. Those were precisely the words she had written.

"Go and sit down now, there's a good boy," Adolphe said. Dazed, I sat down. Adolphe continued:

> Really what I want to do is laugh and leap up and down and stand on my hands and dance around, but you can't do that in prose. So I will have to begin from the beginning; I shall just simply say what happened and

leave you to judge. Not "judge," because I hope you will understand from your hearts what I am about to say and not need the interfering lucidities of your minds.

When I think of us, Adolphe and Charles, I think of a plait—one of Sister Mary's plaits. Joined at the top, divagating in the middle, and then tied—just—at the bottom. I am going to be vainglorious and truthful and say: I am the central one around which you two prance and pother and entertain each other (and me). Without me you would be, as the Americans say, out to lunch.

"Out to *lunch*," drawled Adolphe. "I'm never even *up* at lunchtime."

"Well," I said, "this is certainly the style direct."

"You ain't heard nothing yet."

"Listen to us," I said, "chattering frightenedly . . ."

"Sacred and scared are only one letter apart. The sacred makes one scared."

Adolphe and I looked at each other and smiled.

Adolphe-as-Anna went on:

I came to Pondicherry after Mahabalipuram. I had heard of the ashram of Sri Aurobindo and I thought I would see what it was like. Also I have to admit that I was nostalgic for Paris, for French bread and straight French streets, and I'd been told you could get real brioches here. You can. And the streets are long and empty and white and very French. And there is a hotel called Hôtel de l'Europe where waiters with only slightly provincial accents serve *vin blanc*—at a price. I think this is probably the oddest place I have ever been in—Pierre Loti redone by Duchamp.

You won't be surprised that I hate the Aurobindo ashram. *Hated* it. Those pasty faces in white. Holy slugs feeding themselves in silence. Both Sri Aurobindo and the Mother are dead and their presence is remote, if here at all. I have kept my ear to the ground, and the rumors of corruption and worse seem very plausible. The town hates the ashram too and there are frequent riots . . . Understandable when you realize how rich the ashram is. Only ten minutes' walk away from the *samadhi* there are hovels and canals of shit. The ashramites don't give a prayer.

I was about to leave when I met Jean-Christophe. He was standing in the food queue in front of me, reading Jaccottet's translations of Hopkins. Charles, remember you gave them to me four birthdays ago? Jean-Christophe's thin, ugly, squint-eyed, in his early thirties, and interesting. We got into a huddle and talked in whispers. Here you can talk *only* in whispers.

"What in god's name are you doing in this morgue? What can you possibly have to learn from all these walking corpses?"

"I'm not here for them," he said, and then stopped abruptly. "Are you really interested?" he said. "Or are you just playing?"

Usually, as you know, that's the sort of question that makes me instantly frivolous, but this time I said, "I have not come to India to play."

"We shall see."

Something in his tone angered me so much that I walked out of the dining room. Damn all these religious freaks, I thought. Tomorrow I am going to Bombay, and good old honest corruption.

He ran after me. "Anna," he called out, "I apologize."

I could go on with the touching intricate drama of our friendship, but it would serve no purpose here.

Jean-Christophe told me as we sat by the sea why he was there. He had come initially to live in the ashram; found it as hollow as I did; but then . . .

"Fasten your seat belt," said Adolphe.

He had stayed, he told me, because he had met a very extraordinary young girl. She was from a village in Andra and had been brought to Pondicherry by her protector—a somewhat suspicious smiling plump character called Vilayat. She was only eighteen, but she had what he called (studying my face) "great powers."

"What sort of powers?"

"Why don't you come and see for yourself?"

"I'm leaving tomorrow."

"Cancel it. Come once, You can go the day after if nothing happens."

"What is supposed to happen?"

He ignored my question. "You must meet her. There are very few people who know about her, about ten of us. There is—and there will be—no ashram, no apparatus. Just a small house where she meets us every evening. Where we go, rather." He was stuttering.

"What do you *do* there?"

He laughed. "What do you expect me to say? Levitate? Change into spirits? Astral travel? We meditate in silence."

"Meditate in silence with an eighteen-year-old village girl. You have to admit—"

"It sounds mad. Yes. But the world has boring versions of sanity and madness. Surely you have discovered that."

"Does this wonder-woman speak?"

"In Telugu."

"So you don't even know what she says."

"Look, Anna," he said, "every reply I give you will be absurd if you continue to ask absurd questions. Everything I say will only make you think I've lost it if you approach this—"

"I've heard all this before," I said. "I was in India in

the late sixties. I've lived through the guru number. It bores me to death."

"Good. She is not a guru. She couldn't care less for being a 'teacher' or a 'master.' She doesn't want disciples. She doesn't want a place with white walls and white fat ex-bank managers strolling around it scratching their asses."

"She just wants you to sit in front of her in silence every day between six and seven."

"Five and six, actually."

We smiled.

"Okay," I said. "You seem authentically absurd to me. I'll come tomorrow. But don't expect anything."

"Oh, I don't expect *anything*," he said.

I was rather disappointed.

"You realize," he said quietly, "that I have told you nothing at all about her."

"You have told me she is a young village girl, she speaks Telugu . . ."

"I've told you nothing at all about her," he said more loudly and emphatically. "Nothing. You can't speak about people like her. Words cheapen her."

I thought him a sort of holy simpleton. He had told me earlier that he taught English literature in the South of France. All those pimpled provincial faces had driven him loopy.

That is what I thought then, not with affection. And now I have to ask you to accept that what he told me was true, truer than he or I can express. What do you say to that? "Anna has lost her marbles. Anna is a fool. Anna is mad." Say what you bloody well like with your mind, but listen to me with your heart.

"She's *really* got it bad," I interrupted nervously. "When Anna starts talking about the heart . . ."

Adolphe glared at me and continued:

I went to see the girl next day. That was a week ago. I have been every day since, and each day my experience of her has been deeper.

If you think I'm going to write it all down here, you've got another think coming. Charles would just steal the juicier phrases for one of his novels, and Adolphe would make a huge wonderful joke. No, my friends, I know you too well. You will have to come and find out for yourselves.

I am not joking. I have never been more serious, more *absolute,* in my life. Never. And I warn you that if you do not come—I realize I must sound bossy and hysterical, but I don't give a damn—if you do not come, you will miss everything.

This girl, Adolphe and Charles, is not just a village girl with "powers." She is the incarnation of the Mother on this earth. She is preparing the new world.

I look at my hand writing that. I hear the sea lapping outside the walls of my room. I realize that I might have written the stupidest, most blasphemous sentence a human being could write. But I stick by it. What I have seen and heard and felt and *known* in these last days gives me that right.

I will tell you what I have seen when you come. I will not trust the love of my soul to words.

I am waiting for you. I will not leave Pondicherry. If you come now, you can be in time for the New Year. What have you got to lose?

Anna

Adolphe stopped. "Anna adds this," he said, "in a postscript":

I was in the ashram library yesterday. I came across a book called *Conference of the Birds.* Do you know it? I opened it at random and came on this passage.

You've seen an active spider work—he seems
To spend his life in self-communing dreams;
In fact the web he spins is evidence
That he's endowed with some farsighted sense.
He drapes a corner with his cunning snare
And waits until a fly's entangled there,
Then dashes out and sucks the meager blood
Of his bewildered buzzing dying food.
He'll dry the carcass and then live off it
For days, consuming bit by tasty bit—
UNTIL THE OWNER OF THE HOUSE
    ONE DAY
WILL REACH UP CASUALLY TO KNOCK
    AWAY
THE CUNNING SPIDER'S HOME—AND
    WITH *HER* BROOM
SHE CLEARS BOTH FLY AND SPIDER
    FROM THE ROOM.

(My capitals and italics.)

                      Anna

"Is that it?" I said, after a long pause.

"Is that it?" Adolphe mimicked me. "Is that *it?* It's quite a lot."

"What on earth are we going to do?"

"I booked the flight this morning. In three days' time. Enough time to get the first set of injections."

"You're going?"

"*We* are going." Adolphe paused. "Either Anna is mad and in great danger, or she is onto something momentous. Something the revelations of these last months have been leading to. In either case we must go to her. Natch. Do they still use *natch?* I had this wonderful English lord once who said *natch* all the time. You should have seen his pectorals."

"But, Adolphe . . ."

"Why not die in India?" He put his hand over my mouth. Then he added, "Life is becoming so *very* interesting I have decided to postpone my demise for a bit."

"Who will look after the flat?"

It was the lamest question imaginable, and we both at once roared with laughter. Adolphe began to cough. A spasm of pain crossed his face. For a moment I thought he was going to fall.

"Just drama. Don't be taken in. Abdul always said I would die *without* seeing . . . whoever she is. But the old sod was wrong. I shall break that silly old karma across my legs like an old chair." He coughed again, louder and longer this time. "I'm going to go, you know. I'm going to go. I'm *going* to *go*."

"So you believe in what Anna has written?"

"Has she ever lied to us?"

"She might not be aware she is lying. She might be lying at some level she does not even know exists."

"Come off it, Charles. That is all so *intelligent* and stupid. I like the motif of this young village girl myself. I've always had a soft spot for the working classes."

"*Adolphe.*"

"Look, you poltroon, if she really is the Mother she isn't going to mind a joke. She's probably dying to laugh a bit."

"So you really *are* going."

"You are coming too."

He said it as if spelling out words to a child, very slowly.

"You must be joking."

"You have to. You're not going to let Wondergran loose in India on his own. My god, how could you be so ungrateful?" Adolphe looked at me slyly. "Apart from anything else, how could you bear to miss the fun? Think of the novels in *this*."

"*Adolphe*."

"She probably gets a bit bored with the Silent, you know. Likes a scribbler or two about to sing her praises. Why shouldn't you be that scribbler? It's a menial job, but no more so than any other literary posture." He pronounced *posture* to rhyme with *sewer*.

"Adolphe, you make a great merchant for the Divine. A Rothschild for God."

"That's the sweetest compliment you have ever paid me."

The doorbell rang. Abdul swept in.

"Oh god." Adolphe leapt to his feet. "It's six."

"Five fifty-nine," said Abdul.

"What now?" I said, my head buzzing.

"We are going to see the Tibetan. He's in the catacombs, as I told you. We've found out where. We're going to say goodbye."

"You are going to say goodbye," said Abdul in a sad voice.

"You mean you are not coming with us?"

"No," he said. "One of us has to die here in Paris." Abdul shrugged and swayed.

"You have chosen?"

"I have chosen. I am tired."

The two men embraced.

"Do you think we'll be together next time round?" Adolphe asked. "I hope so. I'm at my very best with you."

"I'm not sure."

"Don't spoil this affecting little scene by criticizing me. If you manage now to love me entirely, you may not even have to live with me again."

"Will you two stop this, please," I said, exasperated. "Reincarnation chic is too much."

"Remember that line. You'll be needing it. And now to the catacombs. Didn't someone say that in *Spartacus*? Some adorable muscled murderer with white teeth?"

"Then what did you do?" Anna asked Adolphe.

We were sitting in Anna's room in Pondicherry. It is bare, with only a small wooden table, a bed, a window that opens onto the sea. Anna was in a white cotton dress, looking thin but well.

"First we all, Charles, Abdul, and I, went to the place Georges Cain—where else?—walked hand in hand three times round the Flora, and placed a wreath of orange roses at her feet. Charles fed Prajna some fresh herring. Abdul did a very dangerous-looking rumba among the sarcophagi. I took my battered old cassette along, so we had Maria singing 'Casta Diva.' The La Scala 'fifty-five performance. La Divina at her most divine. One goddess singing to another! What a farewell to the old world! What an invocation of the new! The tape crackled, of course, but too much perfection is vulgar.

"Then we went down into the catacombs, through a manhole in front of the École des Mines. It was grisly, darling—dank, reeking of meths and urine. Abdul guided us to Blue-Eyes. He was in the room called Chambre Z, sitting in the corner, meditating. He didn't want to talk. He looked wonderful. I told him about your letter, and that we were leaving for India. He chuckled."

"I had never really believed the Tibetan existed," I said. "But he does. As we talk he is there, transmuting his cells in the smelly heart of Paris. He does have blue eyes, just as Adolphe said."

"Never ever disbelieve me again."

There was a silence. A warm wind off the sea filled the room. Adolphe and Anna looked at each other.

"I wonder who is walking in the place Georges Cain," Anna said.

"What time is it?" Adolphe asked in a frail, slightly quavery voice.

Anna smiled. "It is four-fifty. In ten minutes you will be with Her."

ANDREW HARVEY was born in India and educated in England. He is a Fellow at All Souls College, Oxford, an Assistant Professor of Humanities at Hobart and William Smith Colleges, Geneva, New York, the Literary Editor of *Normal*, and the author of *A Journey in Ladakh*. He has written seven volumes of poetry, including his most recent collection, *No Diamonds, No Hat, No Honey,* and three volumes of translation. His first novel was *One Last Mirror.* His second, *Burning Houses,* was published in 1986 and is the first part of a trilogy of which *The Web* is the second. Mr. Harvey is based in Paris.